WINCHELL AND RUNYON

The True Untold Story

Trustin Howard

D1737723

Hamilton Books
A member of
The Rowman & Littlefield Publishing Group
Lanham · Boulder · New York · Toronto · Plymouth, UK

Copyright © 2010 by
Hamilton Books
4501 Forbes Boulevard
Suite 200
Lanham, Maryland 20706
Hamilton Books Acquisitions Department (301) 459-3366

Estover Road
Plymouth PL6 7PY
United Kingdom

Library of Congress Control Number: 2010922926
ISBN: 978-0-7618-5130-1 (paperback : alk. paper)
eISBN: 978-0-7618-5131-8

Θ™ The paper used in this publication meets the minimum
requirements of American National Standard for Information
Sciences—Permanence of Paper for Printed Library Materials,
ANSI Z39.48-1992

TABLE OF CONTENTS

PREFACE

My name is Trustin Howard. I am a television and movie writer. I recently happened to stumble across what I believe is a little-known one-of-a-kind story.

Although many books have been written about Walter Winchell and Damon Runyon as separate entities, with just one or two paragraphs devoted to the other, few know the real story of the slow, bittersweet bonding of these two legendary journalistic giants.

Even television biographies and the recent cable movie about Winchell conveyed just one dimension, and failed to capture the gargantuan proportions that can only come from combining the lives of both men.

Runyon, the "Guys and Dolls" creator, was about 12 years older than Winchell, and was already big-time when Winchell came upon the scene. Maybe that is why the titan Winchell, whose weekly radio show numbered over 30 million listeners, always had a deep-down respect for Runyon and always felt a little smaller in his presence.

Their era put them both in the center of World War II, gangsters, show biz, sports figures, comedy and tragedy. And yet, behind all the headline events, there is a very human and touching story of two men who started out as adversaries, and ended up inseparable.

I have had much experience writing about people's lives. When the ABC Network, Lever Bros., and Ralph Edwards revived "This Is Your Life," I was chosen to write such memorable episodes as Jonathan Winters, Andy Griffith, "Hee-Haws Junior Samples, Phylis Diller, and the classic Bette Davis show, which was the highest rated show of the revised series.

I was also quite pleased with the reception of my first book, "My Life With Regis and Joey" which chronicled my rare experiences as a television writer. However, I now feel that "Winchell and Runyon" is the ultimate of a bigger-than-life story that has to be told.

I thought long and hard as the best way to recount the events. I believe by using an abundance of actual dialogue, this slightly different approach can place the reader more firmly in the center of the unfolding situations. And by reliving yesteryears happenings as though it were just taking place, should also embellish the story. This book is based on public records. However, I was made privy to some personal notes of a Broadway insider who was a confidante of Winchell in that great reporter's twilight years. Possibly, because his life was close to the end, he seemed to reveal his innermost secrets to his Broadway pal.

I am amazed at how few of these startling episodes have ever been exposed to the public.

I use a portion of that heretofore concealed information as a basis for this book. I hope you enjoy the reading as much as I enjoyed the writing...

ACKNOWLEDGMENTS

To my darling Bootsie
who, when the chips were down, always said,
"Yes, you can."

...and to Stephanie for her
constant words of praise,

...and to all these wonderful people
who gave me the confidence I needed
to feel I could write,

Joey Bishop
Regis Philbin
Paul Orr
Eddie Hookstratten
Dick Rosenbloom
Bill Carruthers
Ralph Edwards
Kip Walton
Stephen Pouliot
Bob Banner
Michael Brandman
Lou Alexander
Richard Bernstein
Bob Hope
...and on my musical side,
Marshall Robbins
Jimmy Haskell
Lou Chudd
Cliffie Stone
Ken Nelson
Faron Young
John Mercer Jr.

Ginger and Johnny Mercer
ASCAP
Imperial Records
Warner Bros.
Capitol Records
...and the Rockabilly Hall of Fame

DEDICATION
Thank You and God Bless You, Joey

In almost everyone's lifetime in order to reach some portion of success, someone has to say, "Yes." That person for me was Joey Bishop. Whatever I have done or will ever do as a professional writer, I owe to Joey Bishop, the last member standing of the famous "Rat Pack."

I had been a nightclub comic, working the great clubs which gave the selective patrons their greatest form of entertainment - dining, dancing, and a show. These nightspots were not the Comedy Shops or Comedy Stores. They were the Royal Palaces of Show Biz.

In New York, it was the Copacabana, the Latin Quarter, and La Martinique. Chicago had the Chez Paree, and Hollywood had Ciro's, Mocambo, and later, the Crescendo. Throughout the country, every major city had two or three class nightclubs, and every top hotel had a floor show.

Some of the great performers that starred in these regal palaces were Milton Berle, Sophie Tucker, Joe E. Lewis, Jackie Gleason, Harry Richman, Martha Raye, Tony Martin and Danny Thomas.... The second echelon consisted of Joey Bishop, Tony Bennett, Alan King, Lena Horne, Jack Carter, Sid Caesar, and Pearl Bailey.... The next wave gave us Shecky Greene, Buddy Hackett, Bill Cosby, Phylis Diller, Martin and Lewis, Don Rickles, Kay Starr, Lenny Bruce, Joan Rivers, Billy Daniels, Dick Shawn and Sammy Davis Jr.... Of course, along with dazzling chorus lines, great standard acts filled out the shows. These acts included dance teams, acrobats, novelty acts, tap dancers, and young singers and young comics, all trying to work their way up to headline status. And along with all the smaller clubs around the country, show biz was flourishing.

However, in the early 60s the Vietnam War had started and the mood of the country was changing, and suddenly these wonderful nightclubs with their upbeat talents were being replaced by coffee houses, and singers with one guitar and a hundred sad songs.

Just like talking pictures replaced silent movies, and television replaced radio, these great nightclubs, so many of which I worked, were disappearing faster than casino chips at a Las Vegas crap table.

In fact, some of my last engagements as a young comic were on the West Coast. I shared the stage with Kay Starr at the Casbah in South Los Angeles. I was the opening act for Billy Daniels at the Crescendo on Sunset Boulevard, and I costarred with Buddy Greco at Facks in San Francisco.

However, by 1966 the nightclubs were all gone and the greatest era of entertainment was over. There were also other casualties. As the hippies moved in, comedy and laughter was moved out. In fact, Dick Shawn went to dramatic school trying to learn how to be unfunny. Singers who sang with big bands and their huge arrangements were now trying hard to make it with a couple of guitars. The long shadow of the Vietnam War also nailed television and the variety shows were all being cancelled.

The only nightly TV show that was still providing some laughs was NBC's Johnny Carson "Tonight" show. Johnny always had 10 to 14 writers who came up with a good 12 minutes for Johnny's nightly monologue. Johnny was the all-time champion of late night, and though other shows had tried to make a dent, after 6 to 13 weeks they fell by the wayside. Joey Bishop, who was a member of the famous Rat Pack, was guest hosting a night time show for three straight nights, and when Sinatra, Dean, Sammy and Peter Lawford showed up the ratings went through the roof. Suddenly, the ABC network thought that maybe Joey might be able to give Johnny some competition. They made a deal and in early 1967 they began publicizing the show that was to start in June.

Paul Orr who was the producer of the highly successful Jack Paar Show was hired to bring his team out from New York to hopefully do the same thing for Joey. For some reason, I thought that it would take a nightclub comic to write for a nightclub comic.

At this period, like 99 percent of the comics, I was out of work, and it was only a couple of comedy records and a few small movie parts which kept me from putting up the "Work for Food" sign. However, somehow I managed to get a meeting with Paul Orr whose offices were at the William Morris Agency.

Paul was a gentle soul who gave me time to try to double-talk him into the fact that I was a writer. Although, other than writing for my act, I had never done any professional writing. He even allowed me to play my comedy record which he seemed to enjoy. If the show had been handled by a strictly Hollywood producer, they would have thrown me out of the office. Paul told me they were going to hire five writers and my chances were very slim, but if I wished to send in some material, he would try to have Joey look at it. That was about all I could ask for, and I figured I would never see this wonderful gentleman again.

The show was a William Morris package and they handled dozens of comedy writers. The independent agents were also trying to get their clients placed, and it was like a shark feeding frenzy to fill those five writing spots. I didn't even have an agent, and if it were a horse race I would have been a million to one. But show business makes you punchy, and every couple of weeks, instead of doing a high dive off the Golden Gate, I would write up some material and send it off to Paul.

One day, around the middle of May, I get a call from Paul Orr. He says, "Joey would like to meet you." The call would be equivalent to the Publisher's Clearing House knocking on your door on super-bowl Sunday. I didn't know Joey and we never really crossed paths. I was from Chicago and worked mainly around the mid-west, Joey was strictly a New York and eastern comic. However, Joey did headline a nightclub on the near northside of Chicago called, "Vine Gardens." On that same street, six blocks away, a 17-year-old kid was doing two shows a night, six nights a week, as the comedy emcee at a hot little club called, the "Cuban Village." The kid was me, and nobody knew I was still going to high school during the day. I'm sure Joey was never aware of me, but now I was going to meet him without any idea of what the future would hold.

When I walked into Joey's office I noticed he had a lot of pages in his hand and it looked like my material. He seemed cordial, but there were no smiles. He had me sit down and immediately began reading my gags aloud and rating them. He said, "Good-Fair-Good-Nothing -- Now that line is brilliant." I thought it was mediocre, but "go figure." He then asked if I felt I could come up with fresh gags five nights a week. I said, "I could," then he mentioned different subjects, saying, "Give me a gag about that or that." I'm sure he wanted to see if I could think on my feet. My nightclub background helped me and I was able to come up with some lines without freezing. At the end of this nerve-shattering session, Joey gave me a long look which seemed like an eternity, and I thought this is where he says, "We'll be in touch." But he didn't say that, he said, "Go down the hall and have Elliott make up a contract for you." I have always noticed that those that hit it big in any field have great instincts, and Joey's instinct must have said, "Give the kid a shot." I am certain it was the same scenario for his picking of Regis Philbin to be his sidekick. And years earlier, when Joey starred in his own sitcom, he took a longshot chance on another would-be writer, his name is Garry Marshall. Joey was a rebel and he never bowed to the advice or pressure of the network or even his own agency. In my case, I didn't have one credit and they all must have advised against me, but Joey was his own man and never tried to endear himself to his agency, network or sponsors, and that was the only reason I had a job.

I met and joined forces with the rest of the writing staff which consisted of Elias Davis, and his partner, Dave Pollack, Jim Critchfield, who came over from the Bullwinkle series, and Don Sherman, a very close friend of Joey's. As the show rolled into gear, I realized that Joey did not like writers, but that was understandable. Joey came from the nightclub world where every top comic had a 30- to 40-minute routine that they did nightly. It was their bread and butter - they knew where the laughs would come, and even knew which lines would draw applause. And now, television ate up the whole routine in one or two days. The fact that comics like Joey, Jackie Gleason, Sid Caesar, needed writers to help them was an affront to their comedy manhood. They felt that they had become just readers and they hated it. I remember talking to an old Jackie Gleason writer, who said, "We used to push the material under the door and run." And, if you'll notice, Mel Brooks, Sid Caesar's writer, still jumps when he hears a loud noise.

Johnny Carson had a whole different attitude about comedy. He came from the disc-jockey world. He was never uptight, he left everything up to his dozen writers, and if he got a laugh he found it thrilling.... Joey had to hear a laugh every time he talked. And so, for Johnny it was a pleasure, and for Joey it was constant pressure which came tumbling down on the writers.

After the first 13 weeks, Jim Critchfield was gone. During the next 13 weeks, his pal, Don Sherman took a four-week gig as a comic. I inherently knew that bigtime New York comics like Joey, Gleason, Caesar, and Berle, hated all competition, they were like gladiators who survived. I saw a TV show where Jerry Lewis tried to over-talk Milton Berle. Berle immediately put his hand in Jerry's mouth and grabbed his top teeth. Lewis couldn't talk, and he learned that you never step on a Milton Berle line. That is why I never mentioned to Joey or anyone near the show that I was ever a comic. When the next option cycle came up, Don Sherman was gone so fast and with such deliberateness, many of us claimed we didn't know him.

The writing staff was now down to Davis and Pollack...and I. The three of us managed to keep the show rolling for several months, and then Joey tried to bring in more writers. The problem for many of the new writers, was the fact that we did not write as a team. Everyone had to turn in their separate papers to Joey, who read them all and knew where every gag was coming from. And though many of the writers had great credits, they could not keep up with the nightly pace, and writers were coming and going faster than customers at the bunny ranch.

In a short time we were back down to three writers, Elias, Dave and I. We managed to help get the show picked up for another year. During the early portion of the following year, I happened to be walking down Vine Street for my lunch break when I ran into Joey. He said, "Davis and Pollack are gone." I thought, "Oh no." He said, "I'm bringing in a bunch of new writers and from now on, you're going to be my head writer. Work with these new guys and keep your stuff coming."

For the next couple of months I worked very hard with every new writer from the major shows and sitcoms, but once again, they could not seem to handle the pitching of a nightly show. Their type of writing was just not in sync with Joey's standard. He needed a certain type of gag for his particular delivery. And for the next year and a half I was forced to write for the show by myself. During that period, the show was picked up for another two and a half years, which meant the show would now run at least four and a half years. I was drained, but the moral support I got from my pal, Regis Philbin, kept me going. As we were honing in on our third year of success with ratings a close second to Johnny Carson, Joey called me into his office. He said, "I'm bringing in a new writer/personality who will become my sidekick in a whole new format." I said, "What about Regis?" He said, "He'll still do straight announcing at the top of the show." I had never given Joey any static, but I just couldn't hold back.

I said, "If you make any change in the format, we'll be off the tubes in 90 days." Joey shot back and read me out, also reminding me "Trustin, I've got 18 months on my contract and this will be the best thing I have ever done."

The writer/personality that Joey was talking about shall remain nameless, but doing his thing for the Don Rickles show got it cancelled in six weeks. I also knew that when viewers get comfortable with a show as they did with Johnny Carson and Ed McMahon, and Regis and Joey, you had better leave it alone. Anything that breaks a viewer's comfort zone can be disastrous. Plus the fact that Joey was bringing in a proven non-talent to take over for Regis in a whole new type of format left me panicked. I pleaded with many of the ABC brass to try to talk some sense into Joey. But his same stubbornness which gave me a job, would not allow his decision to be changed.

It was option time and within the next few days I got my usual telegram. But this time, instead of saying, "Your option has been picked up," it said, "You're services are no longer required." Maybe he was mad because I had challenged his decision, or maybe he decided to dump me all along. Nevertheless, my prediction was wrong. I said, "The show would be gone in 90 days," - it was cancelled in 42 days. The show was a train wreck. The show fell faster than Marie Osmond during "Dancing With the Stars." ABC bought out Joey's contract, and he never hosted his own show again.

So many have a tendency to remember the firing, but never the hiring. And how that hiring may have brought so much good into one's life. Joey gave me a career when my other career was gone. Because of Joey, I went on to write some of the great "This Is Your Life" shows. My shows included the lives of Phylis Diller, Jonathan Winters, Andy Griffith, Hee-Haw's Junior Samples, and the highest rated show of the series, Bette Davis. Because of Joey, I even ended up producing TV shows, and Joey gave me enough confidence to write a book, and even be honored with a lifetime membership into the Writer's Guild. When all doors had closed for me, Joey opened a new door, and gave a busted out comic - three straight years of work and a whole new life. No person could do more...

Thank you, and God bless you, Joey Bishop.

CHAPTER ONE
**The journey into one of this country's
most exciting and unforgettable eras – begins...**

This is the story of two men - Walter Winchell and Damon Runyon - who owned Broadway. Broadway was the heart but these two men were the beat. Two fierce literary competitors, each protecting their own turf, and yet, their turf was the same.

They wrote about Babe Ruth and Lou Gehrig and Yankee Stadium.

They wrote about Jack Dempsey and Joe Louis and Maxie Baer and Madison Square Garden. They patrolled Park Avenue and were the first to gossip about the rich and famous.

And they also made celebrities out of broken-down characters who called **The Bowery** their home.

They touted Harlem as the "in" spot for the white highbrow clientele -

- and they championed the careers of the young talents that came out of the Cotton Club and the Apollo Theatre.

They wrote about the mob and gave hoodlums personalities - and were trusted by gangsters who wouldn't trust their own brothers.

They publicized the Palace, the Ziegfeld Follies, and Radio City Music Hall - and applauded the stars - but they gave as much space to the million and one stories about kids with broken hearts and blistered feet.

They gave you the lowdown on stagedoor Johnnies who conned the small town beauties with promises that would never be kept.

They wrote about the Copacabana, and Texas Guinan's, and the Latin Quarter, and the rounders who had it - and those that didn't. They took you inside the Stork Club, and Toots Shor's, and the Club Twenty-One, and made you feel like you were hobnobbing with the hoi-polloi - and they gave you the scoop as to **who** was doing **what to whom**.

They wrote about Lindy's, and Reuben's, and the Stage Deli - where everyone took second billing to a corned beef sandwich.

They sympathized with the dime-a-dozen songwriters and song-pluggers of Tin Pan Alley who sang their hearts out for that one hit.

They took you to Belmont Park and wrote about *Seabiscuit* and *Man O'War* - and about hundred-pound jockeys like Eddie Arcaro and Earl Sande who made two-thousand-pound animals run like the wind.

Yes, they made New York the Big Apple - but they were the core. And what was the background of these two literary giants?

Well, Walter Winchell was the kid who sang on the corner for pennies with his two pals, Eddie Cantor and Georgie Jessel.

He started with a throwaway rag called *The Vaudeville News*, and he evolved into being the most dynamic, fearless, provocative reporter on the scene - His radio show, which had an audience of over thirty million listeners every Sunday night - made him the mightiest force in molding public opinion.

And who was Damon Runyon? Born in Kansas, reared in Colorado, Rode the rails, mingled with outlaws, became a messenger for a whorehouse, worked for his father's small-town paper. Would rather bet a horse than eat. Finally went east, and eventually evolved into what most people said was the best newspaper reporter in the world.

To Runyon, Broadway was a huge playground where he observed the joys and hopes, the troubles and tragedies, of this potpourri of characters he affectionately called - the guys and dolls.

And what was the relationship of these two bigger-than-life men? Well, it was a love/hate relationship - two proud men who kept each other at arm's length - and yet, the quiet love and respect they had for each other could not be denied.

But to better understand the life and times of these two competitors - we have to go back to Nineteen Thirty-seven - NBC Studios, located in Rockefeller Center, New York, New York.

Winchell's 15 minute Sunday night broadcast, which is sponsored by "Jergen's Lotion," is preparing to hit the radio airwaves. Sunday night finds 30 million listeners eagerly awaiting Winchell's spellbinding words.

As always, there is a wild flurry of people running in and out of the studio bumping into each other. A lady brings in a pitcher of hot coffee and cigarettes and sets them on the desk in front of a huge leather chair. A desk microphone plus telegraph key are already in place.

The phones keep ringing. A woman at a smaller desk with a typewriter keeps picking up the phones. She yells into one of them, "I got it. I got it." And then she types. She picks up another ringing phone - and screams, "No. He's already used that."

The big clock on the wall reads 7:57.

A man with a script in his hand is rehearsing with the other hand cupped over his ear. He is the announcer.

The director and his assistant are sitting in a small glass-enclosed cubicle preparing for the show.

A man in a business suit is standing behind them - he is the apparent sponsor, he seems nervous - he looks at his watch and blurts out - "Where the hell is he?"

The director calmly answers, "He'll be here. He just loves photo finishes."

The assistant yells over his mic, "One minute."

The announcer takes his place in front of the floor mic, he stiffens up and starts clearing his throat.

The woman takes the phones off the hooks.

Suddenly, the door opens and in flies Walter Winchell. He wears suit, shirt and tie, and his trademark hat.

As Winchell sits at his desk, the woman pulls the last sheet of paper out of her typewriter. She runs over to Winchell's' desk and lays out 5 sheets of paper side-by-side in front of him.

Winchell seems to speed read the papers while rating them to himself, "Good. Good. That's good, Why, that no-good-son-of-a-bitch."

The clock on the wall shows seconds to a straight-up 8.

The director picks up the count over his mic, "O.K. everybody, standby. Five-four-three-two-one," and he points his finger at the announcer.

The announcer velvets, "And now ladies - Jergens Lotion, for the hands that are as lovely as you are, and for the gentlemen who hold those hands, we present the world's most famous syndicated columnist - Walter Winchell.

Winchell loosens his tie, and pushes his hat back on his head. He starts tapping his telegraph key nervously - it sounds like Morse code - he then continues on with the most famous verbal logo in broadcast history -

"Mister and Missus America and all the ships at sea - let's go to press.

Dateline: Hollywood. David O. Selznick is still looking for his Scarlett O'Hara to play opposite Clark Gable in "Gone With the Wind." Some are saying Joan Crawford has the inside track - others are laying five-to-two on Barbara Stanwyck - but this reporter says, keep your eye on a young English filly from across the sea. Her name is Vivien Leigh. I'll repeat, Vivien Leigh, spelled L-E-I-G-H. Sorry, Louella, but I've probably scooped you again. **Ha!**

Dateline: Somewhere in the Pacific. Amelia Earhart, that great lady pilot, is still missing. The search is still on - but I would suggest that our government talk to the Japanese. I have a feeling they know more than they are saying. Tell them Winchell does not trust them - uh-uh - you never know what they are thinking.

Dateline: New York. Damon Runyon, that small-time writer - you know, the one that writes like the guys and dolls of Broadway talk - dropped another bundle at Saratoga. The horse came in last. Damon, when you want inside information - do what the rest of the world does - come to Walter. That's Walter, Damon. Will he ever learn?

"And now, on a more serious note. That little house-painter, Adolf Hitler, that excuse for a human being who now rules Germany, is continuing to play havoc with certain segments of that country. His band of Nazi gorillas is destroying homes and businesses of many of Germany's good and decent citizens. They are being robbed, raped, and killed - and many are just plain disappearing. The little dictator has made statements which make me think he is not going to stop at Germany's borders. America - there is smoke and fire on the horizon. Do you hear me America? Keep your eyes and ears open.

"And that, Mister and Missus America, winds up another Winchell until next Sunday night. And so for Jergens Lotion, and with lotions of love, I remain your favorite newsboy, Walter Winchell, telling you to take care of yourself - 'cause if you don't, nobody else will.

"God bless you and goodnight."

CHAPTER TWO
Damon Runyon Tells One of His Stories

After his broadcast, Winchell constantly winds down at his private booth at Lindy's Deli. He usually sits alone, but he does sign a few autographs. However, most of the regulars respect his privacy.

Shortly thereafter, a serious man brushes by Winchell's table. He is Damon Runyon. His smiles are few and far between. He is older than Winchell, but he is very dapper with wardrobe that is extremely immaculate. Yet, he seems very aloof, and there is an aura of mystery that surrounds him.

He practically passes Winchell's table giving him no recognition. It is Winchell who yells out, "Damon, Damon Runyon."

Runyon remains independent and cold, "Oh, Hello Walter."

Winchell warmly suggests that he sit down and join him. But Runyon ices him with, "You know I have my own booth."

Nevertheless, Winchell presses on, "Come on, Damon what the hell - it's Sunday night and we're both alone. Let's split a corned beef sandwich. And I want to hear what happened to you at Saratoga."

Runyon looks at his watch, "Well, I suppose I could sit with you for a couple of minutes."

Winchell seems pleased to get the conversation started, "So, Damon, I hear you did a complete tap at the track."

Runyon finally responds, "Well, you heard right, Walter. I started out with some pretty good winners, but then I blew it all on one race."

Winchell is thrilled to say, "What happened?"

Runyon comes up with one more excuse, "It's a long story." Winchell not letting up, "I've got time." And he happily settles in to hear a story from a man whose stories have fascinated millions.

Runyon does not talk Brooklynese. He's a wasp who has written about the people of the streets so long - that when he tells a story, it is just natural for him to talk like he writes. He never tries to be funny.

He starts to relate. "O.K. Well, the past few days I'm at the track with Bruno the Strangler."

Winchell tries to add to the conversation, "Oh, I know Bruno" - and he shows his thumbs as though he is choking someone - "the guy with the thumbs?"

Runyon gives him a quick "right" and continues on.

"Well, it seems that Bruno won a three-year-old colt by the name of *Billy Boy* in a crap game outside of Queens. And he tells me this horse is doing beautiful things in the morning workouts. He is running six furlongs like *Seabiscuit*. And so Bruno figures if he can find a race with perfect conditions - this will be the closest thing to a sure thing since the boys were laying eight-to-five Big Vinnie wouldn't live out the week."

Winchell chimes in, "Oh, I remember that - thirty-six bullets."

Runyon tops him, "No, thirty-seven - they found one in his big toe. Anyway, we're running up a pretty good bankroll - and we're going to bet it all back on *Billy Boy* in the seventh. Bruno has got him running against six females and it looks like a lock. The odds are holding up at four to one - which means that for every fin we get back a double-saw."

Winchell agrees, "A twenty buck profit for a five investment is not bad."

Runyon back into his story, "Right. Now, as they get ready to go into the starting gate, *Billy Boy* is pawing the ground and he's snortin' like a dragon. And we figure this son-of-a-bitch really wants to run. And we go crazy making last-minute bets - we're pulling money out of our shoes. Of course, not being veterinarians, we do not realize that all that pawin' and snortin' are the actions of a young stud in heat."

Winchell getting the gist of the story, "Oh, no."

Runyon continues, "Oh yes. However, the race is off and running. And everything is working perfectly. A couple of fillies go to the front but we're not worried 'cause we know they're going to tire themselves out - and *Billy Boy* is going to nail 'em in the stretch. And sure enough, at the far turn he starts digging in. However, at the back of the pack is a young maiden by the name of *Senorita Sonia* - a beautiful horse but she can't run a lick. And so as they hit the stretch, instead of *Billy Boy* heading for the finish line - he heads for *Sonia* - and the next thing we know - *Billy* is humping her at the eighth pole."

Winchell gives him a heavy, "Oh, no."

Runyon gives him a heavier, "Oh, yes. So while *Billy Boy* is getting screwed - so is everybody else that bet on him. Which only goes to show you, Walter - there's always a new way to get beat at the track.

"Well, I've got to run. I've got to work on the column. By the way, I happened to turn on the wrong station and I heard the last part of your broadcast tonight. Now you know I'm not fond of you, Walter, but I fully agree with what you had to say about that little German asshole."

Winchell is really touched. "Thank you, Damon. I can't tell you how much I appreciate that. You know a lot of people in this country are buying what he's saying. And every time I hit at him I make more enemies - but I know if we don't nip him in the bud a lot of our boys are going to have to pay a heavy price later on."

Runyon gives Winchell one more unexpected kudo, "Well, keep at it Walter this is one time I think you're right."

CHAPTER THREE
Hitler Was On the Move –
But Some of Our Kids Thought He Was a Nice Guy

Winchell was right. Hitler's evil deeds were well underway.

His blitzkrieg of Europe had started with his invasion of Poland – September second, Nineteen Thirty-Nine. But America turned a blind eye to what was the beginning of Hitler's master plan of world domination.

However, here in the United States thousands of Americans seemed to believe in the garbage Hitler was espousing.

They held German bund rallies in most every major American city – and they were held together by that one common denominator – ethnic cleansing –

Anti-Semitism was not only running rampant in Europe – but it was taking hold in this country.

Our people were dangerously divided on this frightening issue. Hitler's adage of divide and conquer was working beautifully.

He even sent over uniforms for young American children – consisting of short pants, brown shirts, and swastika arm-bands – in both countries he called them Hitler Youth.

America was standing idly by – while Europe was beginning to crumble and we were being infected within.

CHAPTER FOUR
President Franklin Delano Roosevelt
Meets Walter Winchell

W inchell is urgently summoned to the White House by President Franklin Delano Roosevelt.

He is greeted by Miss Tully who shows him into the Oval Office. Roosevelt is seated behind his desk as he welcomes the reporter with that same warm wonderful smile that has helped light up America during the dark days of depression. He beckons, "Sit down here. Right beside me."

Roosevelt thanks Winchell for coming in on such short notice. Winchell assures the President that it is his pleasure.

Roosevelt immediately compliments Winchell by letting him know that he's a loyal fan.

Winchell returns the compliment by saying, "That goes double for me, Mr. President."

The President slowly starts to get to the nitty gritty of the meeting. "I must say, I am constantly amazed at your wealth of information."

Winchell humbly answers, "I have a lot of good friends, sir, who try to keep me up-to-date."

The President subtly digs in, "I note you seem to be fighting your own personal war with the Germans. What is your gut feeling about that situation?"

Winchell opens up with as much restraint as possible in front of a man he deeply respects. "We have a very divided nation, Mister President. Hitler is hitting at the worst instincts of mankind. By using the Jews as scapegoats, he has built a solid base in Germany, and he's gaining huge support in this country as well."

The President's wheels turn as he listens intently to every word.

Winchell continues on. "I'm sorry to say, many of our senators and congressmen seem to agree with him, and they refuse to believe that he's a ticking time bomb who poses a great threat to our country. There's not a doubt in my mind that this Jewish situation is just a prelude to a madman who wants to take over the world."

The President digesting Winchell's words to make sure of where he is really coming from, "You are Jewish, are you not, Mr. Winchell?"

Winchell answers in the affirmative.

Roosevelt continues to probe. "Is the anxiety you feel about this Nazi movement largely because you are Jewish?"

Winchell gives him his absolute heartfelt answer. "No, Mr. President, it is because I am an American."

After an extremely long thinking pause the Commander-in-Chief makes a very important decision. "From now on, Mr. Winchell, I want you to work very closely with Naval Intelligence and the FBI. Coordinate your sources of information with theirs. Also, I'm going to start holding weekly briefings with my advisors and the Chairman of the Joint Chiefs of Staff and his officers, and I would appreciate your presence."

Winchell's mouth opens in somewhat of a shock. He expresses how deeply touched he is by the president's vote of confidence in him. He also mentions that he hopes he won't be out of place surrounded by all that brass.

The President's next directive is quick. "You won't have to feel out of place. Today, I'm drawing up a letter that will commission you

Lieutenant Colonel in Naval Intelligence. Of course, wearing your uniform will not be mandatory, but it may make you feel more comfortable at the meetings.

The reporter is ecstatic, claiming it is the greatest honor he has ever had.

The President who is known for his marvelous sense of humor, asks Walter, do you know why Hitler and his Nazi thugs are like a porcupine?"

Winchell shakes his head, "No."

The President is delighted to give him the punchline. "Well, they are all soft and mushy on the inside, but they got thousands of pricks on the outside."

Winchell ends this most marvelous encounter with laughter and heartfelt salute.

CHAPTER FIVE
William Randolph Hearst Meets Damon Runyon

Meanwhile, the famous newspaper publisher, William Randolph Hearst has set up a meeting with Damon Runyon.

Hearst starts to explain the reason for their important conference. "Damon, when your pal, and mine, Arthur Brisbane died, he left our papers with a terrible void." Runyon acknowledges that Brisbane was one of the greatest newspaper columnists that ever lived.

Hearst doesn't mince words. "Damon, I'll get right to the point. I enjoy the column you write for the *American* – I like it fine, but I understand your contract ends in two weeks. I also know they want you to continue on – but I'd like you to come over and write a general column for our King Features syndicate. And of course, we'll double your money."

Runyon is extremely pleased by the offer, but he states his doubts. "Gosh, Mister Hearst, I'm very flattered but I'm not sure I can write that kind of a column. I just focus in on the characters of the street. You see, my style of writing is to make people laugh, and to sometimes tug a little at their hearts. I'm not so sure I can write the same kind of column that Arthur Brisbane did."

The publisher gives him carte blanche. "Then write it anyway you want. Just be yourself. I honestly feel that our newspaper syndicate will open up a dimension of readers that you've never had before. I do believe it would be a tremendous career move for you."

And Hearst extends another plum. In fact, we'll expand the column. I like the idea of laughs, and we can call it "The Brighter Side."

Runyon is interested and happy with the title, but he forewarns, "There might be some tears."

Hearst assures him he likes the idea of comedy and pathos, and he extends his hand for a deal making agreement. Runyon clasps his hand – and "The Brighter Side" is off and running.

CHAPTER SIX
Legs Diamond Puts the Bite on Al Jolson

W inchell is making his usual rounds of his nightlife safari. He manages to get a seat at Al Jolson's late night performance. No matter how many times you see Jolson, he constantly captivates, and Winchell applauds and stands up with the rest of the audience as Jolson thrills the crowd with such favorites as *"Mammy," "April Showers,"* and *"Swanee."*

After the show, Winchell goes backstage to congratulate the singer. He is full of compliments for the man most people feel is the greatest entertainer of the day.

They make a few minutes of small talk when Jolson changes the mood. He confesses a very weighty problem to his pal, Winchell. He explains that Legs Diamond is trying to put the bite on him for fifty G's.

Having heard of Legs Diamond's antics before, Winchell responds with, "Why that small-time son-of-a-bitch."

Jolie further explains, "He says if I don't come up with the dough – he's gonna hurt me real bad."

Winchell asks the automatic question. "Does he have your marker? Do you owe him?"

Jolson answers in the negative, explaining, "I've never dealt with him but he wants me to call it a loan."

Winchell calls it extortion.

The singer asks Winchell's advice. Winchell lets him know that with these kinds of guys – once you give them that first buck – they'll bleed you to death.

Jolson admits he's scared. He has heard that Legs Diamond plays rough, and he's only given the entertainer three days to come up with the money.

Winchell tells his friend that he has an idea, and he is going to make a call to try to get the small-time gangster off his back.

A frightened Jolson thanks him in advance for anything that he can do.

The next day, Winchell makes an important call...

"Mister Costello, please – Tell him it's Winchell. Hello Frank – Legs Diamond is putting the muscle on Jolson for fifty big ones. I know Legs is a punk– but Jolson is scared. You'll do that for him? Oh, you'll do it for me. Thank you, Frank – I owe you, yeah," and he hangs up.

Winchell quickly calls another number...

"Hello, Al – this is Walter. Somebody's going to intercede for you – forget who – just keep your nose clean and play dumb. You're off the hook. No, no – you don't owe me anything Just keep singing those songs and that will be enough. I love you too. O.K., bye." and he hangs up.

Jolson never heard from Legs Diamond again.

CHAPTER SEVEN
**For the First Time Winchell and Runyon
Have a Heart to Heart**

Winchell enters one of his favorite nightly haunts, Reuben's Restaurant. Upon arriving, he always asks Morty the Maitre 'd who is in the restaurant.

Morty names the celebrities. "Bert Lahr, Lillian Roth, Rudy Vallee – and oh, Damon Runyon."

Winchell is always excited when Runyon is on the scene. He walks to the journalist's booth and feigns surprise when he sees him. He tells Runyon that they happened to give away his booth, and he asks if he can join him.

Runyon, who is sitting alone, says, "I suppose I can make room."

Winchell tells the writing legend how much he enjoys his new column. A suspicious Runyon asks, "What's the punch line?"

Winchell assures him, "No punch line. It seems the larger column is making you delve deeper into your characters – and your stories are more fulfilling."

Runyon really seems to appreciate the compliment and comes way down. "Hell, Walter – the guys I rode the rails with could tell you better stories than mine."

Winchell refuses to buy into his humility. "Come on, Damon – nobody puts words together better than you."

For the first time, Winchell and Runyon seem to be having a heart to heart as Runyon continues to open up. "I'll tell you a secret, Walter. I'm like Robin Hood. I steal words of wisdom from the verbally rich, and I give them to the poor."

Winchell is surprised at a truly humble Runyon, "You really don't believe in yourself, do you?"

Runyon continues to tell Winchell his true feeling. "I think I'm just lucky. Not with horses or women, but with writing. I caught a break and I'm hangin' on."

Winchell completely rejects that line of thinking. "Don't put yourself down, Damon. But let's face it, I'd be thrilled if you packed your bags, flew away and left the city to me. But I've got to say, you're one of the most honest and original writers I've ever met – and there is room enough in this town for the both of us."

The first hint of bonding between these two giants begins to show up as Runyon espouses, "You know, Walter – all these years I've always thought of you as a hard-hitting bastard, with no ethics and no scruples – and yet, under that rough, tough facade, I suddenly detect a drop of human kindness – and we are pleased."

Winchell swears him to secrecy. "Well, just don't tell anybody what you found."

Runyon tops him again. "Don't worry, Walter. Nobody would believe me anyway."

CHAPTER EIGHT
Public Enemy No. 1 Still At Large

All the newspaper headlines are boldly glaring the same message. "Public Enemy No. 1 still at large." A further reading explains that – Louie Lepke, public enemy number one, Mister Murder Incorporated, is still in hiding.

In the two years since Lepke dropped out of sight – every hoodlum had been constantly rousted by the cops and the FBI. Life had become so miserable for the mob – they were willing to trade in Lepke for some peace and quiet.

One night as Winchell was coming out of Lindy's, he was approached by a gang member. A big guy partially hiding in the shadows tells Winchell that Lepke wants to come in.

The hoodlum further explains, "He wants to make a deal with someone he can trust. If he walks in out of the blue – he figures some cop cowboy will shoot him on sight. But he's willing to make a deal with someone he can really trust."

Winchell asks the obvious, "Would he trust me?"

The hoodlum says, "I'll talk it out and let you know." And he vanishes into the night.

The following midnight Winchell is sitting at Lindy's when he gets a call on his table phone.

The same hoodlum monotones, "Now, listen carefully – get to the top cop, Hoover – tell him that Lepke will let you set up the meet – but you gotta broadcast on your radio show that J. Edgar Hoover will protect his rights. That way the whole country will know what's happening, and there won't be any slip-ups."

Winchell picks up the challenge. "O.K. I'll do what I can. If Hoover goes for it I'll broadcast it tomorrow night. If you don't hear anything – well, tell Lepke I tried." And he hangs up.

On his following broadcast, Winchell states his position very clearly, "Attention, Louie Lepke, Public Enemy Number One. I am authorized by John Edgar Hoover of the FBI to guarantee you safe delivery if you surrender to me. I'll repeat – Lepke, turn yourself in to Winchell and Hoover will protect your rights."

For the next three weeks, Winchell and Hoover had set up meetings for Lepke to come in – but he was a constant no-show.

Finally, Winchell rushes over to Hoover's suite at the Waldorf. "Mister Hoover, I got another call from Lepke's man last night. He wants to know what the sentence would be if Lepke comes in."

Hoover levels with him. "I'm not a lawyer, Walter – I'm just a cop with a badge – but he's got a heavy sheet on him, including narcotics. It's hard to say which way the jury might rule."

Winchell expresses concern. "I'm afraid if I can't give him an answer he won't come in."

However, well at the end of his patience, Hoover drops the gauntlet. "O.K. I'll fight to get him twelve to fifteen. But the son-of-a-bitch has been giving us the run-around for the past three weeks – So make it clear – if he doesn't come in within the next forty-eight hours, I'm going to order my men to blow him away on sight."

Winchell explains the new rules to Lepke's man and finally sets a definite date.

The time is ten-fifteen p.m. Winchell is waiting on the southeast corner of twenty-fourth street. A lone man comes up to the car. It is Lepke. Lepke thanks Winchell for what he has done.

Winchell tells him that he's glad he showed, and asks him to get into the backseat of his car. He also explains that Mr. Hoover will be waiting for him at twenty-eighth and fifth.

Lepke acknowledges that fact, claiming he just passed him.

Winchell's car finally rolls up to the corner with the country's most wanted fugitive.

Winchell and Lepke both get out of the car, and Winchell immediately introduces Lepke to the head of the FBI.

Both men shake hands as an extremely soft-spoken Lepke, says, "I'm glad to meet you, sir."

Both men get into Hoover's car and drive away.

Winchell watches for a moment, and then drives to the closest public telephone. He quickly gets his number and yells, "Hinson, this is Winchell. I know we only have time for a box bulletin – so listen carefully. Lepke, public enemy number one – just surrendered to the FBI. What do you mean, how do I know? You dumb son-of-a-bitch, I just delivered him."

CHAPTER NINE
The Mafia Evens the Score

Months later, Lepke sends a message from his prison cell wanting to meet with Winchell. The reporter abides by Lepke's request and meets with him on the opposite side of a thin prison screen.

Lepke thanks Winchell for coming, and he asks him if he knew that they gave him fourteen years.

Winchell shakes his head, "Yes."

Lepke gets extremely serious as he says, "Kid, I'm going to ask you a question – and it's very important that you tell me the truth."

A plain talking Winchell assures him, "If I know it – you got it."

An anxious Lepke asks, "What was the sentence you told my go-between, Big Tony Ross that I would probably get?"

Winchell, uncertain where the mobster is coming from, "I told him Mister Hoover would fight to get you twelve to fifteen."

Lepke now makes the conversation clear. "That's what I thought. Big Tony, that double-crossing son-of-a-bitch told me you said four to six."

Winchell is now really concerned. "I'm sorry Lep – but honestly, I told him twelve to fifteen – and I had no reason to lie."

Lepke buys. "I believe you, kid – but if I had known the truth, I never would have come in."

Winchell feels it's important to add, "And you can't fault Mister Hoover either. He kept his part of the bargain."

The convict resigned to the truth, "I know. It was Big Tony – the bastard sacrificed me like a virgin into a volcano."

Winchell is apologetic. "I'm really sorry, Lep – If there's anything I can do, just let me know."

Lepke relieves Winchell with his final words. "You did good, kid, and so did the G-Man. I'll remember that, and thanks again, kid."

A few nights later, Big Tony Ross comes out of a restaurant with a big buxom blonde at his side.

A voice from the dark yells out, "Hey, Big Tony Ross – Lepke wants me to deliver a message to you."

Big Tony turns toward the voice and smiles.

A tommy gun delivers the message, quickly pumping dozens of bullets into the big man.

And, once again, the mafia evens the score.

CHAPTER TEN
**Damon Runyon's Young Wife, Patrice,
Comes to New York**

Damon Runyon is in his New York apartment typing furiously when there is a knock at the door. After two long minutes the knock finally registers and he opens the door. He seems thrilled to see his beautiful, much younger, wife, Patrice.

She reminds him that she has been waiting at the train station all morning for him to pick her up. However, she is aware that when he is writing a column, nothing else truly matters.

It is not the greatest of marriages, because she lives in Florida and he lives in New York. But he claims he can't write about New York if he lives in Florida.

It seems she has come to the big city to give their marriage one more chance.

A usually unemotional Runyon, realizing his first marriage went down in flames, senses that this second marriage is now teetering on the brink. He tries to convey his deeper feelings, "I know this isn't the life you expected – but I do love you, Patrice."

She doubts that he knows what the word love means, telling him that sometimes it seems he doesn't have any feelings at all.

Runyon is quick to tell her that she is always in his thoughts.

She asks the profound question, "What about your heart?"

He explains that since the first day they met, she has had it all.

However, she makes her inner feelings quite clear. "You know,

Damon – I can't take a long distance love much longer."

Damon pleads with her to stay with him for a few weeks. He feels the fun and excitement of the city will work this time, and she can live with him in New York. Undoubtedly, they have tried this before.

She agrees to give Damon and the city one more chance.

He starts his second courtship by taking her to one of his first loves – the racetrack. He excitedly cheers his horses across the finish line while she yawns and gives him half-hearted smiles.

On another night, Runyon is in a serious card game with 3 or 4 of his buddies. Patrice sits alone on the sofa, completely bored as she reads a newspaper.

On still another occasion at 3 in the morning, Runyon is sitting in a cheap restaurant booth, directly across from him a cabbie-type is telling a story. It is obviously an important story, because Runyon is taking notes. However, poor Patrice, who is sitting next to him, has her head on the table. She is completely exhausted and sound asleep.

Another night passes and it is dawn. Patrice wakes up and realizes she is alone. Damon still hasn't come home.

The following morning, Patrice has made her decision. Her bags are packed when Runyon comes out of the bedroom. He is still in his robe and seems confused. Patrice makes it clear, "I'm leaving, Damon. I'm going back to Florida. I realize more than ever that we live in two different worlds."

Damon, not understanding, "That's not true. Your world is my world."

Patrice seems willing to take the blame. "Maybe I'm jealous – jealous of the fact that you find every minute of your day thrilling and exciting. God, you can talk to a bum on the street for an hour and find it invigorating – and you and I can't put together ten minutes of conversation."

Runyon still doesn't grasp. "Gosh, Patrice, I thought you were really enjoying the last couple of weeks, nightclubs, the track, shows – what else is there?"

Patrice gives him the answer. "There's a home and there's children – and waking up and finding the morning – but you put the morning to sleep. You live in a topsy-turvy world, and there's no place in it for me."

A bewildered Damon asks, "But isn't love the equalizer?"

Patrice tries hard to explain. "Yes, I love you. I'll always love you – but it takes more than love and you don't need me. Most of the time you don't even know I'm around. You have a great life, Damon – you're fulfilled. But mine is empty, and I've got to try to give it some meaning."

Runyon still trying hard to grasp. "I wish I knew how to make you happy. I wish I knew how to change. But I don't know any other way. You're right, my life picks up speed at midnight, the racing form is my bible, and to me, a hotel room is home. I'd give anything to be what you want me to be. But if you took those things away from me – I'd have no desire to live."

Patrice looks at him like a child she dearly loves, but she can only sympathetically say, "I know that – and it's sad. But I'm going back to Florida to get some rest and some sanity. And as much as I hate to say this, dear, dear, Damon – our journey is over."

Damon tries hard to straighten up, but he is resigned. "Naturally, I'll abide by whatever decision you make. Maybe I don't fully understand love – but what I know of it is all yours. So, do what you have to do – and thank you for all those wonderful moments you have given me."

He gets dressed and drives her to the train station.

In the next few weeks the newspaper headlines read – "The Damon Runyons Split."

CHAPTER ELEVEN
**There's a Sad Song For Every
Broken Heart on Broadway**

Winchell and Runyon and a couple of other buddies are sitting at the famous Stork Club. A much brighter than usual Runyon, dominates the conversation by describing his day at the racetrack.

"So, it's the last race and I see these two horses that I like. One is called *Lover Boy* and the other is called *Scribe*. So I figure what the hell – I'm a better writer than I am a lover– and *Scribe* comes in and pays thirty-three-twenty, and it ends up being a beautiful day."

Everybody smiles but Winchell.

He asks the other two gentlemen at the table if he can spend a few moments alone with Runyon. The other two men graciously oblige.

Winchell talks to Runyon like a stern older brother.

"I know you'd like to impress everybody with this non-caring attitude about your marriage breaking up – but this happy-go-lucky, beautiful day bullshit doesn't impress me one bit. You're still crazy about the lady, aren't you?"

Runyon comes way down. "How do I win her back, Walter?"

Winchell is a great judge of human nature. He knows how important it is to lend a sympathetic ear while giving a no frills opinion. "You can't. You just torch it out – and when it gets unbearable you've just got to try to replay some of the great memories."

Runyon just can't seem to nail down the idealistic needs of the opposite sex, let alone his own wife. "How is it possible, Walter, that I can communicate with gangsters, hookers, cab drivers – and they all understand me? But the one that means more to me than anybody else – has no idea as to where the hell I'm coming from."

Winchell gives him his street-smart philosophy. "We're complicated guys, Damon. Our work is our life. So there's not much left over for some kind of happy-ever-after payoff. Women like Patrice can't be second best – with them it's all or nothing at all."

Runyon wants to know how Winchell who lives his same kind of life-style doesn't have a problem with his wife, June.

Winchell has a simple explanation. "June is a different kind of a woman. I laid it all out up front. She says she has no regrets and she's never gone back on her vow."

Undoubtedly envious of Winchell, Runyon bemoans his marriage failure in the only terms that truly makes sense to him.

"I guess Patrice and I just faded in the stretch."

Winchell practically lifts Runyon out of his chair, deciding to take him to Tommy Lyman's joint. Tommy Lyman is the singer that has a song for every broken heart on Broadway.

His place is a hangout for those that need a sad song to help them cry in their beer. He also belts romantic ballads when he sees hopeful young lovers holding onto each other.

However, the singer knows that Winchell has brought Runyon in to get as much sadness out of his system as he can. Lyman obliges by dedicating a song to his pal, Damon Runyon. He sings a heartbreaking rendition of "You're nobody 'til somebody loves you."

A grief-stricken Runyon cannot stop the tears from streaming down his face.

The usually cold, unemotional Runyon probably hasn't shed a tear since he was a very small boy. But Winchell knows that sometimes a good cry is the only thing that can really help.

CHAPTER TWELVE
**The Politician's Try to Take Winchell's
Microphone Away From Him**

The war in Europe was heating up – but America was still standing pat.

The isolationists of the America First movement were headed by the powerful Burton K. Wheeler, Senator from Montana.

Many in Congress literally hate Winchell. They resent anyone wielding that much power who is not a politician.

Senator Wheeler takes the floor of the United States Senate to deliver what he feels is a very important mind-molding speech to his political cronies.

"This war is no business of ours. Hitler's army is much too strong – and we cannot allow ourselves to be pushed into a war that we cannot win. The Germans hold no malice toward us. So let the war stay where it belongs – on the other side of the ocean. But I tell you this – these warmongers like Walter Winchell have to be stopped. Mister Winchell has to be taken off the air. And as Chairman of the Senate Interstate Commerce Committee, I do have some small influence over radio legislation, and this day I am going to introduce a bill that will take Mister Winchell's microphone away from him. We cannot allow the American people to be influenced any longer by that peddler.

"I mean – fear peddler."

Winchell is quick to fire back. On his next broadcast he hits the airwaves with both barrels blazing.

"Mister and Missus America and all the ships at sea – Let's go to press.

Dateline: Washington, D.C. United States Senator Burton K. Wheeler has proposed legislation to bar news commentators from programs sponsored by advertisers. It's another shot fired across the bough of freedom of speech. It is a brutal and vengeful act that is meant to seal the lips of anybody with an opposing point of view. Ladies and gentlemen, if this law passes – the advertising field will be under federal control – and every major radio station will have to answer to the Interstate Commerce Committee – not so incidentally chaired by Mister Wheeler.

But I say this bill is unconstitutional. It's a battle that was fought a hundred and fifty years ago – and if and when this case goes to the Supreme Court it should be properly named ....Burton K. Wheeler versus Patrick Henry and Thomas Jefferson – and the court should sit at Valley Forge."

One week later the Wheeler Radio Bill died a quick and quiet death – and Winchell single-handedly saved an entire industry from extinction.

CHAPTER THIRTEEN
Walter, Eddie, and Georgie –
They Sang on the Corner for Pennies

Walter Winchell constantly holds court at New York's world famous Stork Club. His table 50 has become his second office. He has a phone on the table for the calls that constantly come in from publicity people, actors, actresses, sports figures, politicians, even hoodlums, who all want to find favor with the king of newsmen.

They all know that a complimentary blurb from Winchell cannot only mean success in a career, but for hoodlums, it can also create a more sympathetic atmosphere in a courtroom.

This night, the famous owner and host of the Stork club, Sherman Billingsley, meets Winchell at the door telling him that he has taken the liberty of seating a couple of his friends from the west coast at his table.

Winchell reminds Billingsley that he doesn't like surprises. However, when he is told that the two friends are Eddie Cantor and Georgie Jessel, all is forgiven. He practically runs to the table, and all three hug as nostalgia comes to the fore.

These were the three kids who sang on the corner for pennies – and now Eddie Cantor who has five daughters has graduated from vaudeville, to the Zeigfeld Follies, to one of the most successful shows in radio.

Georgie Jessel has also moved from Vaudeville and nightclubs to producing movies in Hollywood.

They both feel that their pal, Winchell, needs a little moral support because of the constant barrage of potshots he keeps getting from the people calling him a warmonger.

Winchell explains to his two buddies that most of the nation doesn't see Hitler as a threat, and people in very high places are buying his bullshit.

The two concerned celebrities ask, "What's going to happen?"

Winchell gives them a frank and sincere answer. "The American people are very fair. They'll see through it. But we're eventually going to be pulled into a very long and bloody war, and we're not prepared. But America always seems to have God as an ally."

Winchell tries to change the gloomy subject and reminds the guys of their young days in Vaudeville. He reminisces, thinking back on how the three kids got their big break and broke into the bigtime act known as "Gus Edwards and the Singing News Boys."

Edwards was a Vaudeville headliner who constantly worked with kids. Just as "Our Gang comedy" was successful in early movies, Gus Edwards found that kids could be equally successful in Vaudeville.

Once the group hit the stage, the adult Edwards had the three kids dressed in caps and knickerbockers with all three carrying newspapers under their arms.

He would then call one kid at a time forward, asking him to put his newspapers down. When the first kid arrived front and center, Edwards would ask his name and how he sells his papers.

The typical answer would be, "My name is Eddie Cantor and I sell my papers in Brooklyn. I sing a little song and everybody buys."

The adult would say, "Show us what you mean." Young Cantor responded by saying, "Hit it, Maestro," and sings *"Toot-Toot-Tootsie"* while the other two kids do a little choreography consisting of mostly hand moves behind him.

The next little boy that was called forward was Georgie Jessel. He explains that he sells his papers in the Bronx and he gets people to buy when he sings his favorite song, *"My Mother's Eyes."* When Jessel sang that song there wasn't a dry eye in the house, and it remained his theme song for the rest of his life.

It should be noted that an older Jessel took a young girl out on one of his famous Vaudeville tours. The girl's name was Frances Gumm. Jessel introduced the young thirteen year old singer as a girl that was headed for stardom. He also felt it was best to change her name for career purposes. He did – and her name became Judy Garland.

The third young boy called forward was Walter Winchell who explains that he was born in Harlem and he loves his country and his flag.

A snare drum would start rolling quietly in the background as young Winchell would patter –

> Amid fields of clover,
> Twas just a little over,
> A hundred years ago;
>
> A handful of strangers
> They faced many dangers
> To make their country grow.
>
> It's now quite a nation,
> A land of inspiration,
> Where bells of freedom ring.
>
> It's your land, it's my land,
> A great do-or-die land
> Where everyone can sing.

The music comes up as Winchell goes into a rousing chorus of –

> America, I love you,
> You're like a sweetheart of mine,
> From ocean to ocean,

For you my devotion,
Is touching each boundary line.
Just like a little baby,

Climbing his mother's knee,
America, I love you,
And there's a hundred million
Others like me.

Copyright: Kalmar & Puck, 1915

Edwards who had left the stage – enters dressed in a World War I Johnny Doughboy uniform waving a big flag as he marches across the stage.

The boys file in single file marching behind him, waving smaller flags and all singing, *"America, I love you."* The band then segues into "Three cheers for the red, white and blue." The four performers march in cadence back and forth across the width of the stage. They finally exit to a wild ovation from an audience that stands up and cheers for a full two minutes.

The reminiscing leaves Jessel with tiny tears filling his eyes. He says, "I believe those were my happiest days. Maybe I still try to relive them by going out with young broads."

Cantor, also sniffling, admits, "If it weren't for Ida and my five kids, I'd go back to those wonderful times in a minute."

Winchell confesses, "I've always been envious of you two guys. You stayed with it and you became stars, I broke my heart trying to hit the big time in Vaudeville – but I just couldn't hit the pitching."

Eddie Cantor can't quite seem to understand this envious confession coming from one of the most influential men in the country.

Georgie Jessel also reminds Winchell, "And Walter, you're still singing *'America, I Love You,'* only you're doing it with your typewriter."

CHAPTER FOURTEEN
"Apple Annie" Causes a Terrible Breach
In the Relationship

One of Damon Runyon's most popular published stories is about a broken-down fruit seller in The Bowery – he named her "Apple Annie."

She constantly sits on a chair behind a small wooden box containing 3 or 4 apples. Some days she waits hours for customers who never show. She has an air of elegance and throughout the terrible despair, she holds her head high.

Damon Runyon is extremely fond of her and respects the pride with which she carries herself. However, she cannot ward off her impending fate, and she actually dies of starvation.

Runyon has been out of the city for a couple of weeks, and has no idea that his story's heroine, "Apple Annie" has passed away.

Upon Runyon's arrival back in the city, he meets with Winchell for dinner at Lindy's. He is also anxious to have Winchell bring him up-to-date on what he possibly missed in the two weeks that he was gone.

Runyon looks extremely dapper and healthy, and proudly boasts that he finally had a good meet at Arlington Park Race Track in Chicago. He also brings regards to Winchell from some of the mob boys in the Windy City.

Winchell tries to fill in the two week gap by telling Runyon that he had a wonderful reunion with his pals Eddie Cantor and Georgie

Jessel. He also seems quite sure that Runyon is aware that Apple Annie died a couple of days ago.

Runyon's mouth opens in shock. He did not know, and he asks what happened.

Winchell unemotionally tells him that he thinks the old lady died of starvation.

Runyon simply cannot understand why somebody didn't do something to try to help her.

Winchell nonchalantly surmises that she never asked.

Runyon blurts, "That's 'cause she was too proud to ask – that wasn't her style. Did you know she was in trouble?"

Winchell explains that he heard something about her being sick a week ago.

Runyon, completely flustered, "Well, why didn't you do something? A couple of bucks might have saved her life."

Winchell levels, "Look Damon, I can't take care of every bust-out in The Bowery."

An extremely angry Damon shouts back, "But she was special. You know what she meant to me."

Winchell asks, "Then why didn't you do something?"

Runyon claims he didn't know.

Winchell, calling him on it, "You had to know – it was in my column."

Runyon is furious, "You don't understand, Winchell – I don't read your goddamned column."

Winchell spitting out this sudden bitter pill, "Well, then maybe it will teach you a good lesson."

Runyon explodes, "I don't need you to teach me anything. You really are what everybody thinks you are – a heartless, soul-less, no good, son-of-a-bitch!"

An equally mad and sarcastic Winchell thanks him for the praise.

Runyon comes up with his final insult, "And you can take your goddamned column and stick it up your ass." And he storms out.

Sometimes when the vibes of two great men collide – it can cause their paths to take an unexpected turn.

CHAPTER FIFTEEN
Damon Runyon Goes Hollywood

Hollywood has been beckoning to Runyon for quite some time. However, he constantly refuses their offers. He is in his warm comfort zone of New York and has had no desire to leave. But now possibly due to his awful breach with Winchell, he has a change of heart and finally accepts the heavyweight proposals from the movie world.

He arrives in the fantasy land of Hollywood and Vine to turn some of his short stories into cinema magic.

He writes and produces "A Slight Case of Murder" which comes from his intimate relationship with thugs, hoodlums and racketeers he knows. It involves a big time bootlegger who goes to his summer home during the racing season at Saratoga. He finds four dead gangsters with bullet holes in their heads strewn out at different areas of the house.

The bootlegger decides to deliver a dead body to the doorstep of four different hoodlums, figuring one of them might have been responsible for the wholesale slaughter. The hectic hilarity of playing musical chairs with four dead bodies makes the movie an instant success.

He writes "Lady For a Day" as a fitting and final tribute to his true-life "Apple Annie" whose narrow daily adventures intrigued him so very, very, much. Frank Capra wins an Oscar for directing.

He writes Shirley Temple's very first hit movie, "Little Miss Marker." A story about a gambler who leaves his kid with a bookie for security. It is the start of the most fabulous child star careers in motion picture history.

Among others, he writes and produces, "The Big Street," a tearjerker about a chorus girl with delusions of grandeur and a busboy who secretly loves her. She is crippled in an accident, and the busboy devotes his love and his entire life in looking after her. The movie stars a couple of new kids – their names – Lucille Ball and Henry Fonda.

And so Runyon takes over Hollywood, just as he did New York.

CHAPTER SIXTEEN
Winchell's War Prophecy Comes True

W inchell's constant warnings of an impending war fell on deaf ears and December seventh, Nineteen Forty-One, the Japanese carried out a sneak attack on Pearl Harbor and an unprepared America. Our naval fleet was practically wiped out.

As the raid was taking place – the Japanese Ambassador and his entourage were discussing peace with our leaders.

President Roosevelt took to the airwaves and declared war on Japan.

Germany and Italy, who had been waiting in the wings for just the right moment – immediately declared war on America, and now we had to battle on two fronts. And a battered and confused America had to pick itself up and enter into long and bloody World War Two.

CHAPTER SEVENTEEN
**New York Without Damon Runyon
is Like New York Without the Statue of Liberty**

Winchell couldn't stand the rupture of his friendship with Runyon. He stated in his column that New York without Runyon was like New York without the Statue of Liberty.

The Japanese attack on Pearl Harbor seemed to be the perfect excuse he needed to swallow his pride and try to cement relations with Runyon. Runyon also seemed ready to forgive and forget.

Runyon is staying at the Beverly Hills Hotel. He is sitting in the lobby when he hears his name being paged for a telephone call.

He picks up the phone and is surprised to hear Walter Winchell's voice. They had not talked since their blowout over Runyon's Bowery Lady.

Winchell uses the earth-shaking excuse to find out if there is any truth to the rumor that Japanese submarines are firing on Los Angeles.

Runyon assures him, "Nah, the little bastards wouldn't dare – Metro-Goldwyn-Mayer would eat 'em alive." Runyon also takes advantage of the moment to find out how things are in the big city.

Winchell tells him that without his ugly face around – things are pretty quiet.

Runyon admits that California is equally boring. Somehow talking to Winchell again makes him more homesick for New York and he discloses, "Dammit, Walter – with this war going on – if it wasn't so hard to get an airplane reservation I'd leave tonight."

Winchell immediately comes up with a solution. "If you are really serious about coming home – I think I can pull some strings and have a ticket set up for you within a couple of hours."

Runyon can't hide his surprise at Winchell's overwhelming power, "Do you really have that kind of power?"

Winchell proves that he has – and that same night Damon and Walter are sitting together once again at the Stork Club.

They both seem happy to have their friendship back on track and really seem to enjoy talking to each other.

Runyon tells Winchell about an unbelievable fact. "Do you know that the nightclubs in L.A. close at midnight? I took a walk at two in the morning and they picked me up for vagrancy."

Winchell reminds him that this is where he belongs, and since he's been gone, the hookers and the pimps feel nobody cares about them.

Runyon gives him a belated compliment. "You really called the shots on this war Walter – you deserve a lot of credit."

Winchell explains, "It was clear to me, but I took a lot of punishment for it...rabble rouser, war crazy bastard.... You tell the truth and people want to destroy you. Go figure."

Runyon tries to clarify, "Well, maybe it goes back to the old kill the messenger bit. But you're a true patriot, Walter, and I find that refreshing."

Winchell truly becomes humble in the rare shower of a Runyon compliment. "You're probably a majority of one, Damon, but I'm deeply touched."

He then comes up with a suggestion that is going to bond these two legends for life. "You know, Damon, I start making my rounds of the city after midnight, why don't you join me? While I'm looking for scoops – you might find some great stories."

Runyon seals it – "You've got a deal."

CHAPTER EIGHTEEN
"The Dawn Patrol"

Winchell and Runyon indeed join forces to find the stories that start unfolding in the middle of the night. They follow fire trucks, squad cars, and even chase ambulances with more agility and determination than the hungriest of lawyers.

In fact, many of their fourth estate peers jokingly plant them with the moniker, "The Dawn Patrol."

Many are the nights that they push each other out of the way of fire enveloped falling debris. Winchell's car radio scanner which picks up police calls quite often helps them get to the scene of the crime long before the rest of the cop brigade. However, their early arrival constantly puts them in harm's way.

Winchell sees a man trying to stab another man who is already on the ground. The reporter jumps out of the car like a stunt man and grabs the predator's arm, while yelling, "Drop it – drop it, there'll be no killing while I'm around."

The sudden surge of adrenaline seems to give Winchell a new found cache of strength. His voice also resonates the authority of some sort of killer force that makes the victimizer run for his life.

The victim cannot stop thanking Winchell, explaining that the man was trying to rob him and the arrival of his powerhouse hero absolutely saved his life. Winchell accepts the accolades like a humble superman. They finally drive the grateful gentleman home, and discuss the night's frightening event.

After reality sweeps in, Winchell looks down at his shaking hands, and says, "Cheez, I could have gotten myself killed. Why would I do that?"

Runyon who is equally shaken tries to remind, "Aren't we supposed to observe instead of getting involved?"

Walter claims, "I just couldn't let that man get killed."

Damon points out, "yeah, but if the other guy tried to stab you I'd have to get involved, and I freely admit that I'm a better writer than I am a fighter. So, in the future, dear Walter – please don't do that again."

They both feel that the incident has cause for a couple of heavy drinks, and they decide to quickly head for the last show at Texas Guinan's.

CHAPTER NINETEEN
"Hello Suckers"

Texas Guinan's is the "in" spot for the mob, the rounders, and the celebs. Texas herself is considered the greatest hostess of them all. Her sarcastic humor is a must see that keeps the joint jumpin'.

Most of the customers think Guinan owns the place – but she is really a front for mob boss Owney Madden.

Madden was brought up in "Hell's Kitchen" and served eight years in Sing Sing. He is one of the big names in New York's underworld, although his outside demeanor is that of a gentleman. Some of the other mob boys that constantly frequent the nightspot are Dutch Schultz, Lucky Luciano, and Frank Costello.

Of course, Texas Guinan insults her audience with equality, and even the hoodlums are not spared. But they just laugh off a Guinan sharp inflicting one liner that could, undoubtedly, get others killed.

Winchell and Runyon arrive at the club just as the band leader introduces Texas Guinan.

She is a nice looking, fortyish blonde who opens every show with her famous trademark, "Hello Suckers." The audience answers back in unison, "Hello Texas."

She gets the laughter started by saying, "Last time I saw a group like this – I was in night court."

The sets the audience up for her first story. "So, I'm out with this big spender – and he takes me to this very fancy restaurant where the waiters speak French – anyway, I think it was French – and the waiter comes over to our table and asks, 'What'll you have?' And the big spender says, 'She'll have a chicken sandwich and a coke'. And I say, 'Wait a minute – I want steak and champagne.' And the Big Spender says, 'Does your mother give you steak and champagne?' And I say, 'No – but she doesn't try to put her hand between my legs either.'

The laughter is heavy as she starts looking around for the patrons she can nail.

She sees an older bald-headed man with a pretty young gal with a perm. The gal is also covered with a huge mink coat. Texas singles them out, "Well, if it isn't Daddy Warbucks and Little Orphan Annie. Sweetheart, I'm glad you finally got rid of that lousy red dress." The audience screams as Texas follows up – "Did you get that beautiful mink coat for being good?"

The squeaky voiced gal is up for the occasion as she yells back, "No, I got it for being bad."

This is the kind of banter that has made the place famous. She catches another couple off-guard. The woman is elderly, dripping with jewelry. The boy is much, much younger and somewhat shy of the sudden spotlight.

Texas hits them with, "Lady, we're begging you – give the boy back to his mother." The lady laughs good naturedly along with the audience as Guinan continues, "Actually, right before the show, the kid came up to me and asked if he should stay with the lady or go to college? I told him stay with the lady. He'll learn more in one night from this old broad – than he could ever learn from four years of college."

The laughter persists as she spots Winchell and Runyon. Guinan acts shocked, "Well, I don't believe it. Look who's here – Damon and Pythias...and once again, Damon is getting Pythy-ASS drunk."

The audience roars as she continues on.

"You all know Damon Runyon – only man I know who bets horses that start in a kneeling position...and of course, my very good friend, Walter Winchell. Winchell never stops talking. One day we went to the beach –and the only thing that got sunburned was his tongue."

The crowd loves it as Texas softens the blow by saying, "Just kidding, Walter. I don't want to wake up tomorrow and find my career is over."

Winchell leads the audience in well deserved applause showing his approval.

Guinan humbly bows, following with, "And now I'd like to present our chorus line of eight beautiful virgins – we used to have ten – but two of the girls went out last night and broke their contracts. Here they are – the Guinan Girls."

The scantilly clad gals come out and sing and dance to the popular hit of the day, "*The Varsity Drag.*"

About halfway through the routine Winchell asks, "Damon, how would you like to go home with one of those cookies?"

Damon gives him one of his profound answers. "Not for me, Walter. I learned a long time ago women make men crazy. In fact, the only time a man is completely sane – is during the ten minutes following an orgasm."

Winchell slowly nods in agreement as the dancing girls wiggle their fannies, the band plays loudly, and the drinks continue to pour.

CHAPTER TWENTY
Winchell Broadcasts One Flash Too Many

Winchell is bursting at the seams to hit the airwaves with his Sunday night broadcast. He has information that he considers a scoop.

To Winchell, the scoop is the most important element of his career. It means getting a hot story out to the public long before any of his competition has any idea of what is happening.

Along with the scoop whether it is written or broadcast, Winchell never lets his readers or listeners forget that their first and best source of information is Walter Winchell. He boasts about that fact, constantly.

The scoop has made Winchell the all-time king of the hill, and though many personalities let up when they reach their goal, Winchell never lets up, he keeps going after that next all important scoop like a man possessed.

And so, this Sunday night, after his trademark opening, Winchell hits his radio audience with "Flash: New York, New York. A bunch of the boys from Chicago are visiting our fair city. You know, the ones with the noses on the side of their faces. I understand Vincent 'Mad Dog' Coll is giving them a lot of problems."

Gangster Owney Madden happens to be seated at his desk listening to the broadcast – while some of the boys are cleaning their tommy guns and pistols. When Winchell says "Mad Dog" Coll they all look up in shock and anger.

Winchell continues on, "The boys no lika da problems – but they should have it worked out in a day or two. I'll be back in a flash with a flash."

The hoodlums are furious, one of them yells "that no-good son-of-a-bitchin' matzo Christ. (Chryst)" This is the ultimate Sicilian put down for any Jew.

Another hood screams, "When this is over I'm gonna nail that Juda bastia (Jew bastard)"–and he bites his index finger and aims his whole arm at the radio.

A couple of nights later a car with two men on the inside pulls up to a drugstore. One of the men is "Mad Dog" Coll. He gets out of the car and goes to a telephone booth directly on the inside of the drugstore right near the entrance.

A hoodlum sneaks up to the driver's side of the car and gets off one shot to the driver's head with a silencer. The driver slumps. Two other hoodlums walk into the drugstore and they blast Coll with tommy guns while he's in the phone-booth.

Winchell and Runyon are sitting at their usual Stork Club table when Detective John O'Brien finds the two newspaper men amid the crowd. The cop brings them important news. "Winchell, I thought you'd like to know – Vincent, the 'Mad Dog' made his last call tonight."

Winchell's eyes pop, asking, "What happened?"

O'Brien tells him that he got pumped in a phone booth on West Twenty-Sixth.

Winchell yells with absolute boyish excitement, "What a scoop. I nailed it right on the money, didn't I?"

The Detective stays level, "That you did – but be careful, kid – you're playing in a very heavy league."

Runyon asks for the full story on the "Mad Dog" moniker.

The Detective explains, "A few years ago, Coll was in a shootout. One of his bullets went into a baby carriage and killed a three-month old infant. He never showed any remorse. He said it was the baby's fault. He laughingly said that the baby was in the wrong place at the wrong time. It even disgusted the other hoods, and that's when they shackled him with 'Mad Dog.'"

Runyon shakes his head in disbelief, "Well the bastard got what he deserved."

The cop leaves as Winchell thanks him for the good news.

Winchell is still excited as he relives the event. "Well, what do you think of that, Damon? I out-scooped all those guys that do this crime stuff for a living...I tell you Damon – there's no greater feeling than getting a scoop – it's better than getting laid."

The phone at his table rings, Winchell picks it up and boastfully answers, "This is Winchell, your crime reporter. What? What? What? Who is this? What are you talking about?" (The line apparently goes dead.)

Winchell's face turns so white, it causes Runyon to ask what's wrong.

Winchell weakly answers, "the mob's got a contract out on me."

An equally concerned Runyon asks if there is anything he can do.

After thinking for a couple of moments, Winchell decides he has to handle this himself. "I've got to go right into the lion's cage. I've got to go straight to Owney Madden and cop a plea."

Runyon wants to go with him.

But Winchell says, "No, No – you stay here. I'm too hot right now. I may never get to him and I've seen these killers in action – they'll spray everyone around me. And Damon, if I don't make it – tell my wife, June – I've always loved her and I'm sorry I wasn't a better husband. And thank you, Damon, for your friendship – and I'd appreciate your saying a prayer for me."

And he leaves.

CHAPTER TWENTY-ONE
Winchell Cops a Plea With Gangster Owney Madden

W inchell makes the long, lonely nightime ride to Owney Madden's Long Island estate. While driving a million thoughts keep dive-bombing the inside of his head and they are all negative. His mind is actually on a runaway merry go-round and it can't get off.

He finally arrives at a place that can be his last living destination. He gets out of the car and slowly walks to the door, his strength is completely depleted, but he tries to straighten up as he rings the doorbell.

A thug looks through the one-way peep-hole. He walks back to Madden who is seated behind his desk in his study, and tells him, "It's Winchell, Boss. I can pop him at the door and bury him in the back."

As always, Madden remains cool-headed. "No, no. Let him in. I want to hear what he has to say."

Winchell, who is ushered to the inside of the mansion is immediately frisked as three other hoods give him icy stares.

Madden tells the boys to leave, but they don't move until he thumbs them out.

He gives the reporter a look of disgust as he says, "Sit down, Winchell. You know, you got a lot of guts coming here. You practically blew the whistle on some of the boys – and the boys don't like it."

Winchell talks for his life. "But I'm a newspaperman, Owney. I don't know if you understand but that's my business. I live on hot stories and scoops. And yet, you know, I've always soft-pedaled for you, and Frank Costello, and Lucky Luciano. I've always set up the Robin Hood angle for you guys. I never let people forget that you give to the church, to the orphans, to the soup kitchens for the poor. I've made you guys heroes, and I would never do anything to hurt you."

Owney seems to accept the reminder, "Yeah, I know that – but broadcasting the Coll thing – a lot of guys are hotheaded dagos, kid – and they all want a piece of your ass . . . and I want to know who shot off their mouth?"

Winchell becomes definite, "You know I can't tell you my source, Owney."

Madden becomes emphatic. "I've got to know who sprung the leak."

Winchell sinks in quiet resignation. "Owney, if you want to take me down, take me down, now – but I can't tell you. It's a rule all newspapermen live by. Just like you have rules and laws, so do we."

Madden, respecting the clam, "I understand that. I have a hunch it's Texas Guinan. She's the only one stupid enough to spill. Just give me a yes or no– and I promise nothing will happen to her."

Hoodlums have the instincts of hunting dogs, and when Madden says, "Guinan" something in Winchell's body language changes, and the hoodlum has his answer. "Yeah, I'm right, it's Guinan. But she's always been good for us – so the promise still goes – nobody's going to hurt her. But we're going to have to zip up around her. Now about you – I like you, kid. You came up hard like all of us. You're gutsy and you're a scrapper.... He pulls out a business card and writes something on the back.... So I'm gonna give you my card. Show it. It means if you're in trouble they'll have to deal with me."

Winchell, taking the card, "I really appreciate this, Owney – but while there's a hit on me, nobody is gonna give me time to show a card. They could blast me right outside your door."

Madden makes a decision. "Yeah, you're right, kid. Aw, what the hell, I'll see what I can do...." He picks up the phone and dials.

"Hello Eddie, it's Owney. I'm making a statement on behalf of Winchell. He carries my card. I know, I know all that – but he's a newspaperman and that's his business. The only one that got hurt was 'Mad Dog' – and that son-of-a-bitch had it coming. Look, this kid with his mouth and his writing has personally swayed Judges and juries for me, and Lucky and Frank, which makes him a friend. We owe him...Well, make them understand. Besides, you know it's bad luck to kill a cop...or a newspaperman. I'm counting on you, Eddie."

And he hangs up the phone.

"O.K. Winchell, I did what I could. I laid my position on the table – but it's gonna take time for my word to get around, and even then, there's always a couple of hotheaded guys that want to make you an example. So, here's my advice. Take a vacation. Get out of town and do it fast, and for your sake, I hope it blows over."

Winchell heeds the advice of a gangster who seems to be sincerely trying to prolong his life. The reporter grabs his wife, June, and before morning they are gone.

CHAPTER TWENTY-TWO
Winchell and Juney Take it On the Lam

For the first time since starting to write his daily column for New York's *Herald-Tribune*, the Winchell column does not appear.

The bold-type newspaper box reads: "Winchell column cancelled due to illness."

The thirty million listeners of his radio program also feel the emptiness. In fact, with the lack of his voice and writing, most of the country's population find it hard dealing with the void. Rumors start taking hold that the great reporter is actually dead.

However, Winchell and his wife, June, are hiding out in a small isolated hotel along the Florida coast. Winchell trusts no one but Runyon with his whereabouts, and only Damon knows the phony name he is using. Other than in New York, few people actually know what Winchell looks like. It is only his radio voice that is familiar to the masses. Nevertheless, he is well aware that if any of the mob gets word of his location, he would most likely have a tommy gun ending. So complete secrecy is in order.

Ironically, for his wife, June, it is a blessing in disguise. To finally have her husband all to herself for any length of time makes her ecstatic.

June is not unlike many wives of professional men who have to share their husbands with the public. Many of those wives can't handle the long days and nights, and even weeks turning into months of loneliness.

But June has hung in. She dearly loves her Walter, and she realizes that she has to keep the empty home-fires burning while her man lives in a hotel room in upper Manhattan close to the action of his life's work. And so these two weeks of being on the lam have been her happiest since their 3-day honeymoon. Winchell also states that he feels ten years younger.

As they sit on the sand of the hotel's small beach, June voices her inner-thoughts, "It's a funny world, Walter, they had to put out a contract on you – so I could spend some time with my husband."

Winchell reminds her, "June, when you're not in a normal business – you can't have a normal life. But we both needed this, didn't we, honey?"

June's heartfelt answer is, "More than you know."

A bellboy walks up and quietly tells the assumed-named Winchell there is a telephone call for him.

The call is from Damon Runyon. He first asks how things are going.

Winchell's answer is, "Just fine. Juney and I are acting like a couple of lovesick teenagers."

Runyon then gets right to the reason for the call. "Walter, I ran into Owney Madden. He told me to tell you, at this point, all seems clear. He thinks the boys have pretty well forgotten – they're into other things. He is also quite certain that his word has gotten around that you are a personal friend, and he feels if you wish, you can come home.

Winchell asks Runyon's gut feelings.

Runyon assures him that there have been no rumblings on the street. He also feels it's safe to come back, but he realizes it's Winchell's decision.

Winchell thanks Runyon for the heads up. The reporter is a well known workaholic who is anxious to get back into harness. Although, he knows June is going to hate the news.

He breaks it to her as gently as possible, "Damon says it's all clear – June, I really think it's important that we leave tomorrow."

June can't hide her emotion, "Damn it, Walter. Can't we just stay another week?"

Winchell tries to calm her down. "Juney, these two weeks have been the greatest. But you know as well as I do – the paper is getting nervous – and you can never let them know that they can get along without you."

June grudgingly agrees, and they seal her understanding with a long passionate kiss.

Two older ladies happen to be passing at that moment. Seeing Walter and June in such a warm embrace, causes one of the ladies to state, "I'll bet they're newlyweds."

June enjoys hearing what she feels is a wonderful compliment. She is pretty well resigned to the fact that what she secretly considers is a second honeymoon is coming to an end. But she still is awfully cute as she looks into Walter's eyes and lets him off the hook. "O.K. Pal, it's been great fun – but I guess it's time to go back to our neutral corners."

Winchell dearly loves her and kisses her tenderly on the forehead.

Winchell and Runyon are back at the Stork Club discussing the events of the past few weeks.

Winchell refers to his close call as a photo finish. Reliving his frightening moments, "I'll tell you a secret, Damon. Even though some of the mob guys are my closest friends they scare me to death. One minute they can be as charming as headwaiters, and the next minute they can turn around and kill you. I've seen it happen."

Runyon adds his own experiences to the conversation. "Yeah, they're a weird breed, all right. They'll kill you for a quarter – and yet, if you give them a hard luck story – they'll lay a C-note on you, and wish you well. Go figure."

Winchell remembering how much hoodlums love publicity, "One time, when I was in Chicago, I got an interview with Al Capone. He said, 'How come you newspaper guys don't write about the good things I do. I've poured millions into this city. I've put money into every important cause.' And he has. So I put a couple of words in the column about some of the nice things he has done. And sure enough, he calls me and can't stop thanking me – a real gentleman. Unless you're on the wrong side of his gun."

Winchell's table phone rings. It's from a publicity man who gave him wrong information. Winchell reminds him, "I told you, ace – I'm not taking any more of your items for three months. I don't care if Rita Hayworth is pregnant. I know I can't keep her from being pregnant. But I sure as hell can stop her from being pregnant in my column."

And he hangs up.

CHAPTER TWENTY-THREE
Runyon and His Dog, Nubbins

Damon Runyon takes his red cocker spaniel, Nubbins, into the pet hospital. The dog has been acting listless and seems to be having trouble swallowing.

While waiting for the vet, Runyon sits on the sofa with the dog lying at his feet. There are also other dogs in the room waiting to be examined.

Nubbins is his pal and he talks to him like he is human.

An older man walks into the office with a cute little poodle. Runyon quietly says, "Hey Nubbins – get a load of the broad – a real beauty." But the dog doesn't look up. Runyon surmises, "You must really be sick."

A woman is leaving the hospital with a large Great Dane. Runyon is quick to say, "He's a great doctor, Nubbins – when that dog went in – he was just a chihuahua." The dog gives him a "bad gag" look.

They both finally go into the office of Doctor Stanley Jones, the veterinarian.

Jones puts the dog up on the table and he examines different parts of his body. He finally opens the dog's mouth, looking in – and especially feeling under his neck. He makes a quick diagnosis. The dog has inflamed tonsils.

Runyon expresses the fact that he didn't know that dogs have tonsils. He also instinctively grabs his own neck, claiming, "I don't like to hear that. I almost died from a tonsillectomy a few years ago. In fact, I still feel it."

Dr. Jones can't understand why Runyon would still have pain. However, as for the dog, he wants to immediately take out his tonsils and keep him overnight.

Getting back to Runyon, the doctor confesses, "Human beings are a little out of my line, but if you're still having trouble I'm willing to take a look."

Runyon laughingly agrees, claiming that a lot of people think a vet is definitely his kind of doctor.

Jones starts to examine his throat, and almost thinking out loud, he is confused by all the lesions that are down there.

Upon finishing the exam, Jones seems quite concerned and he expresses it. "I'll tell you the truth, Mr. Runyon – I don't like what I see. I don't want to scare you, but I recommend that you see a throat specialist as soon as possible."

Runyon, still not grasping the seriousness, suggests that he can lay down with Nubbins and maybe they can get a group rate.

Dr. Stanley Jones is not laughing and he begs Runyon to take care of his throat problem immediately.

Runyon promises that he will, and he tells Nubbins that he'll see him tomorrow.

CHAPTER TWENTY-FOUR
Runyon Checks Into Hospital
(The Heavy Sound of Silence)

Two weeks later, Runyon following the advice of Doctor Jones, sets up a meeting with the famous throat specialist, Doctor Hayes Martin. The specialist finds Runyon's condition much worse than he would have thought, and he feels it is imperative that he operates immediately.

At Runyon's request, Winchell is immediately summoned and he gets to the hospital, as quick as possible. He finds Runyon's room, sees him in bed and asks, "What the hell happened?"

Runyon, still trying to keep it light, "Well, for quite some time I've had this pain in the neck – and all along I thought it was you."

Winchell remains serious. "No jokes, Damon – What is it?"
Damon levels that they found some cancer. He explains that they don't know how far along it is but they're going to operate today and try to get it out.

Winchell shakes his head in disbelief.

Runyon philosophizes, "I think my dog, Nubbins, and I are snake-bit. He blew it three days after his operation. I sure hope I have longer than that."

A nurse and attendants arrive and help Runyon onto a gurney.

Runyon gets more serious and asks Winchell to say a prayer for him.

Winchell assures him that he will, and he clasps his hand, stating that he'll be waiting for him to get back.

As Runyon is wheeled out, Winchell turns away and buries his head in his hands.

The operation takes far longer than expected and Winchell paces the hall for hours like an expectant father.

Finally, Dr. Martin comes out with his forehead thoroughly wrinkled.

Winchell stands frozen as the doctor tells him, "It went far beyond our worse scenario. We tried and tried, but in order to save his life, we had to remove his larynx."

Winchell gives him a look of not understanding.

Doctor Hayes Martin makes it clear. "We had to remove his voice box. It breaks my heart to say this, but the great Damon Runyon will never speak again."

Winchell's knees buckle.

The doctor continues, "And at best, Mr. Winchell, we're just buying time. He may have six months, maybe a year. He just came to us too late."

Winchell asks if Runyon knows.

The doctor explains that he is still under. "But it is important as a friend, you try to keep his spirits up – he's going to need all the help he can get."

When Runyon is eventually wheeled back into his room, both Winchell and the doctor go in and sit at his bedside.

Runyon who is still slightly under, finally opens his eyes. Seeing Winchell, he mouths the words, "Hi Walter." When no sound comes out, he does it again – and again – and again, and when nothing happens he gets wide-eyed and somewhat hysterical as he tries to find his voice.

The doctor asks Winchell to leave for a few moments as he wants to speak to Mr. Runyon alone.

After a long twenty minutes, the doctor tells Mister Winchell that he can go in, Runyon knows.

Winchell's mind goes a mile-a-minute trying to figure out what he is going to say.

As he enters the room Runyon is just shaking his head from side to side in disbelief. He is completely devastated.

Winchell gulps as he tries to find the right words. "I know this is the toughest battle you've ever had. You can stay down for the count – throw in the towel and call it quits."

Runyon gives him a cold stare.

Winchell continues, "Or you can fight back and win. It's up to you. We can still do all the things that you love. We can go to the track, we can go to the clubs – they didn't take away your legs. And most important of all you can still write – they sure as hell didn't take away your brain."

Runyon looks for a pad and scribbles a note.

Winchell reads it. "So you just want to die? Well, that's fine with me. It just gives me another good story for my column...Runyon didn't have the guts to live. It sure isn't the image I'd like to leave with this world, but hey pal, it's your decision."

Winchell is secretly hoping that he is taking the right approach.

Runyon scribbles another note.

Winchell reads. "O.K. So I'm a no good son-of-a-bitch who doesn't understand – All I know is I got two box seats to the Kentucky Derby coming up in four weeks and there's any one of a million people that would love to go with me. But of course, if, in the next couple of weeks, you decide to get your ass out of this bed, I'll hold the ticket for you, but once again, that's your decision."

The wheels of Runyon's mind seem to do a lot of spinning, after an extremely long period, he picks up the pad and scribbles again.

Winchell picks up the pad, reads it, and tries to be as blasé as possible as he answers. I think a horse by the name of *Pensive* is going to win it...I think he's going to be about eight to one. And I'll tell you another thing – you'll probably be here a couple of more weeks, and I'm willing to come in every day with racing forms and we'll bet every track in the country with the bookies. That way we'll warm up and be trigger sharp for the Derby...that is, if you really want to go."

Runyon seems to be giving the offer a lot of thought.

And for the next couple of weeks Winchell keeps his promise. Runyon's room is loaded up with racing forms and all kind of tout sheets. As Runyon scribbles his choices, Winchell keeps dialing and calling in bets for the both of them.

Winchell doesn't go back on his word and Derby day finds Winchell and Runyon at Churchill Downs.

The horses are off and running, and as they finally hit the eight pole of the stretch run – jockey Con McCreary starts whipping feverishly – and *Pensive* crosses the finish line first.

The usually reserved Runyon is so thrilled to have one of his rare winning tickets – he actually hugs Winchell. They both bet heavily on the winner, and like so many of his on-the-target predictions, this time it is Winchell's handicapping that sends them home with a fistful of money.

The two of them truly become inseparable. And as Winchell promised a very sick Runyon, they are constantly at the track, the ball parks, the theatres, the nightclubs, just anywhere they can find some kind of action.

Winchell inherently knows the importance of keeping Runyon busy during this painful and trying time, and he devotes his every spare moment to his newspaper pal.

CHAPTER TWENTY-FIVE
1945 - One of the Most Eventful Years in History

It was now Nineteen Forty-Five. One of the most eventful years in America's history.

In February, Churchill, Stalin and a very tired and worn-out President Roosevelt had their famous meeting at Yalta in the Crimea. It was at this meeting that Russia decided to enter the war against Japan.

However, two months later, on April twelfth, Franklin Delano Roosevelt, America's most beloved, and only fourth-term President, passed away at the age of sixty-three from a cerebral hemorrhage.

Vice President Harry S. Truman was immediately sworn in as America's thirty-third President.

America was winning the war in Europe and our soldiers were moving toward Berlin.

On April thirtieth, the madman Adolf Hitler, who was a step away from world domination, committed suicide in a Berlin bunker.

On May fourth, the German army began surrendering en masse.

An unconditional surrender took place on May eighth. This day became known as V.E. Day – Victory in Europe.

On August sixth, Harry Truman ordered the first atomic bomb to be dropped on Hiroshima.

Three days later a second atomic bomb was dropped on Nagasaki. Japan surrendered on August fourteenth.

On September second the Japanese formally surrendered. This event took place on the *U.S.S. Missouri* and September second, Nineteen Forty-Five became officially known as V.J. Day – Victory over Japan.

Our boys began coming home from all four corners of the earth.

And America was getting ready to settle down to peace in our times.

Winchell is sitting alone at his Stork Club table. A quietness permeates the room.

Owner of the Stork Club, Sherman Billingsley, walks over to chat with him. "I hate to say this, but since the war has ended – the action sure has died down."

Winchell agrees. "I never knew silence could be so loud."

Sherman laughs. "That's the truth. By the way, how's Damon?"

Winchell tells him. "He's in constant pain. Sometimes the pain is so excruciating – I can actually feel it.

He can't sleep so I take him on my rounds every night to get his mind on something else. I try to knock him out, and sometimes he dozes a little bit."

Sherman is forced to say, "You're a good friend, Walter."

Winchell admits, "It wasn't always that way, but I guess I learned to love the guy."

Billingsley marvels at the fact that he still seems to write a hell of a column.

Winchell adds his admiration. "He writes on instinct. And no matter what he's going through – his words never lose that edge. Truthfully, I don't know how many of us could do that. Well, I've got to go pick him up."

Sherman still in awe. "Give him my best,"

Winchell assures him, "I will, Sherm, I will."

CHAPTER TWENTY-SIX
The "Dawn Patrol" Sees Action Again

W inchell drives up to the front of Runyon's hotel to pick him up for their nightly rounds. It is a freezing night with actual blizzard conditions.

A doorman walks out a decrepit Runyon who tries to aid himself with a cane. Winchell jumps out of the car to also assist him.

He double checks with Runyon to find out if he really wants to go, and if he is warm enough.

Runyon nods "yes" to both questions.

It's two-fifteen in the morning as Winchell takes his place behind the car steering wheel and Runyon sits close to him. Their special radio is turned on to get police calls.

While driving the calls start coming in. "Car Twelve. Check domestic quarrel at one-oh-two-one Seventh Avenue."

Another call comes in, "Car thirty-four. Check on fist fight in front of Houlihan's Bar on West Eighth."

Suddenly a radio call comes in that makes Winchell perk up. "Signal Thirty-Signal Thirty-Twenty-Fourth Precinct-Twenty-Fourth Precinct. Three white men in white cab last seen speeding south on Manhattan Avenue from a hundred twenty-first street. Proceed quietly. Use caution. They are armed."

As Winchell makes a fast U-turn, he yells, "This is it, Damon. This is why we do this every night – the action. No movie can match the real thing."

Damon reacts with eyes widening, looking forward to taking part in the hunt.

Winchell's car pulls up to a red light and stops at a 116th and Manhattan. Several white cabs are also stopped.

Winchell remains excited as he bellows, "Think of it, Damon. They could be in any one of those cabs. I'll stay close to them – and you keep your eyes open for three guys."

Damon's eyes squint, searching as many cab interiors as his vision allows.

An energized follow up police call is broadcast. "That signal. Thirty in the twenty-fourth – the white cab's last three numbers are oh-three-oh. Three white men wanted for holdup in the twenty-fourth. Proceed cautiously, no sirens, no red lights – they are armed."

Winchell and Runyon hear another frantic call come in. "Charlie–Charlie – This is Rosselli. We've spotted the cab parked at a hundred first street and Manhattan. Bill and I are moving in – send back up."

Officer Rosselli and his partner, Bill, get out of their squad car and draw their guns. Bill goes around to the passenger's side, and Rosselli takes the driver's side. He notices only one person sitting in the cab on the driver's seat.

Rosselli points his gun at the apparent driver and asks, "Is this your cab?"

The driver answers "Yes," and slowly and carefully pulls out his license.

Rosselli asks, "Where are the three guys you picked up at a hundred twenty-first street?"

The cabbie is quick to answer, "Those guys scared me to death. They all had guns – one had a shotgun. They went into that building there." And he points to a close by three story building.

Back-up police cars start flying in from all directions with red lights glaring – and sirens blasting. Winchell and Runyon also pull up and get out of the car. Runyon walks a little more steady, but Winchell takes no chances and holds him quite firmly.

Other cops are carrying Klieg lights not as yet lit.

A janitor comes out of the building amid the ruckus to find out what is happening.

Suddenly a barrage of gunfire rings out from the roof. Everyone takes cover, but the poor janitor is hit in the groin, forcing the cops to instinctively fire back up at the roof.

A detective yells for an ambulance, and then screams, "Hit the roof with the lights."

As the Kliegs light up the roof, the detective grabs a bullhorn and yells. "You up there – We're coming up. Drop your guns – raise your hands or we'll shoot you on sight. I repeat – drop your guns – raise your hands or we'll shoot you on sight. Come over to the edge where we can see you. Come on boys, you can't win this one."

The lights reveal two of the hoodlums putting their hands up and standing near the edge of the roof.

The detective yells at police sergeant McCrane that he will go up to the roof and bring the two hoodlums down. He orders the sergeant to search the building for the third man.

Sergeant McCrane, who has a slight Irish brogue picks out a couple of men to help him with the search. When he spots Winchell and Runyon, he yells, "So, you two boys want action, huh? Well, you come with me."

The two reporters are extremely excited as they are invited to follow the police veteran McCrane.

Despite the difficulty, Runyon noticeably tries to straighten up.

The McCrane group goes from door to door, and every door brings out people with different degrees of emotion.

An old woman in a robe and curlers almost faints when she sees pointed guns. But that doesn't stop the cops from going in and searching her apartment.

An older man comes to the door shaking with apparent palsy. What he sees makes him shake more profusely. The cops push the shaking man aside and thoroughly search his apartment, but come up empty.

One of the next doors reveal a younger man in his long underwear. His apartment is completely dark. The man cannot stop yawning as McCrane walks in and hits the light switch. He immediately sees another man in bed sleeping like a baby.

The sergeant asks, "Who is he?"

The man says, "I never saw him before."

The answer doesn't make sense to anyone and one of the cops immediately aims his gun at the yawning man.

McCrane goes over to the sleeping man and pulls the covers off of him. He then pushes his hands under the pillows looking for weapons, but finds nothing. The man still remains sleeping.

Finally, McCrane starts pushing the sleeping man, yelling at him to wake up.

The man opens his eyes and seems shocked to see cops surrounding him.

McCrane asks the man's name and where he lives.

The confused man says that his name is Ted Peters and he lives right here.

McCrane follows up with, "Well, who's this guy?"

The sleeping beauty answers, "How should I know? I've never seen him before."

McCrane bellows, "One of you guys is lying through your teeth."

The veteran policeman thinks for a moment, and then asks, "Peters, where are your shoes?"

Peters answers, "Where I always keep them – under my bed." And he points to them.

McCrane picks up the shoes and puts his hand in each shoe. Thinking out loud, he quietly says, "ice cold."

He then asks the other man, "Where are your shoes?"

The man answers, "Where I always keep them – under my bed."

McCrane goes through the same motions, putting his hand in each shoe.

The act forces a smile to appear on his face as he says "Oh, you darlin – they're as warm as me dear old mother's heart. Cuff the son-of-a-bitch and take him away. Peters, you're off the hook."

Winchell is in awe as he compliments the policeman. "McCrane that was sensational. The guy that's been sleeping all night has ice-cold shoes, and the guy that pulled the holdup and has been running around all night has shoes as warm as hell."

McCrane finalizes it. "That's the ticket. Well, anyway you got your scoop Winchell. We just captured the Park Lane Gang."

He then looks at Runyon with warmth and tenderness.

"And Damon, take care of yourself, hear? It's much too cold to be out on a night like this – you get yourself back into a nice warm bed."

Runyon smiles and nods, "Yes."

Winchell and Runyon seem very satisfied as this night's activity ends for them.

As Winchell drives Runyon home, the older man falls asleep on Winchell's shoulder. He snores lightly as Winchell keeps his shoulder in place as not to disturb him. He also drives with one hand using the special knob on his steering wheel. This lessens his movement and allows Runyon to get a bit of his much-needed rest. Winchell seems very pleased as he quietly says, "That's good. Sleep tight Damon, sleep tight."

CHAPTER TWENTY-SEVEN
Winchell and Runyon Reminisce

In the next few days, Runyon gets progressively worse. He is shot up with morphine to ease the pain and give him some bearable moments. Winchell as always is at his bedside and a twenty-four nurse is on hand.

Winchell tries to cheer him up by reminiscing.

"Those were the days, weren't they Damon? Remember, when I was writing for The Vaudeville News – I was completely tapped out, and I had to go to the bank and borrow a hundred bucks for my rent – and you're already a big-timer – and I run into you and you take this new dummy kid to a big party and the liquor flowed, and the food was great, and when we got ready to leave – you say, kid – do you have any money? And I pull out this precious hundred-dollar bill – and you took it and gave it to the waiter. When I told my wife, June, she couldn't stop crying. The next day I had to go back to the bank and plead for two hours for another hundred. Do you remember that, Damon?"

Damon writes something on a pad. Winchell good naturedly reads.

"Sure, big deal – so with interest – now you owe me two hundred."

Damon weakly laughs and enjoys as Winchell continues.

"Damon, do you remember the first time we took Sherman

Billingsley to Lindy's? You're gentile, but he was really gentile. He ordered a hot corned beef on whole wheat bread with mayonnaise. The waiters were swearing at him in Jewish, and he thought they were speaking Japanese."

Damon puts his hand over his mouth as though he's really chuckling.

Winchell keeps up the banter. "By the way, I quoted you in the column yesterday. Winchell and Runyon have the perfect friendship. Winchell can't stop talking – and all Runyon can do is listen."

They both enjoy. Damon writes – Winchell reads.

"Oh, yeah, I remember that – Sherman didn't allow anybody in the Stork Club that wore white socks, and Ernie Hemingway always wore white socks – so we asked, how did you get in? He said it was easy – and he pulled up his pants leg and said, I just didn't wear any socks. What a character."

The sweet nostalgia is at the fore as Winchell remembers. "The best one of all was when Sir Alexander Korda gave you a check for a hundred thousand dollars to write a movie. And you showed me the check – and then you threw it on the floor. And I said, why the hell did you do that? And you said, I wanted to see if it would bounce."

Damon smiles and slowly closes his eyes.

Eight days later, on December tenth, nineteen forty-six, the great Damon Runyon closed his eyes forever.

CHAPTER TWENTY-EIGHT
Everybody Loved Damon

A devastated Walter Winchell takes the airwaves on his Sunday night broadcast to pay a final tribute to his pal, Damon Runyon.

"Good evening, Mister and Missus America and all the ships at sea – Let's go to press.

"A very good friend of mine – and a great newspaperman – (Winchell's voice breaks) – Damon Runyon – was killed this week by the number one killer – cancer. It is odd that even though his voice was taken from him two years ago – right up to the very end his words remained the voice of the guys and dolls of Broadway that he loved so very much.

"Let's fight back – let's do something about this terrible killer. I am going to set up an office at NBC, Rockefeller Center, here in New York. Will you please bring in a penny, a nickel, a dime, or a dollar, or send it to my attention.

"This money will go into a fund, and I promise no expenses of any kind will ever be deducted. And from now on we will call this fund – The Damon Runyon Cancer Fund."

Winchell's broadcast seems to touch everyone. Runyon's loyal followers start digging in to somehow pay back some of the love that Runyon displayed for them in each and every one of his columns.

The waiters and waitresses of the many restaurants along the great whiteway all contribute. Especially, the guys and dolls of

Lindy's who all tearfully remember Runyon's quote. "There are only two kinds of people in this world. Those that eat at delis, and the others I wouldn't care to know."

On his next broadcast, Winchell gives his listeners a cheerful update.

"Mister and Missus America and all the ships at sea – let's go to press.

"Last week we started the Damon Runyon Cancer Fund, and I'd like to report some of the results to you. Many of the people wanted to remain anonymous – but I know Damon would want me to mention some of his pals.

"Frank Costello got us started with twenty-five thousand dollars. Bugsy Segal added another eight thousand.

"The management, the owners, the trainers and the jockeys of Belmont Park all pitched in and gave us a check for fifty thousand dollars. I know Damon would have been thrilled, for this is the first time he's ever scored at the track.

"And this one Damon would really appreciate – Joseph "Socks" Lanzia – who's serving eight to ten in Sing Sing – sent in two hundred and fifty bucks that he collected from his fellow inmates – and they're all embarrassed that they couldn't send in more.

"And on that same note – one time big-timer George Scalise, who's doing three to five and working in the prison laundry room sent us his entire life savings – a hundred thirty-nine dollars and ninety cents. Thank you, George. Damon knew you guys would never forget him.

"I also want to thank a couple of grammar school kids from P.S. Four who brought in nine thousand pennies which came from also every kid at that school.

"Time doesn't permit me to single out everyone. But in one week, two hundred and fifty thousand dollars has been donated in Damon Runyon's name, and much more is coming in. At that rate a cure for cancer will not be far away.

"And so until next week, this is your favorite newsboy, Walter Winchell, saying, as you must know, in his own way Damon Runyon loved each and every one of you. And so that old adage still holds

firm. There is no greater gift than to love and be loved in return.
"God bless you and good night."

CHAPTER TWENTY-NINE
Winchell Reads a Letter

Two weeks later Winchell is about to fulfill his promise to Runyon to scatter his ashes over his beloved Broadway.

This final ceremony involves five people. Along with Winchell, they are Damon Junior and his wife. He is a son from Damon's first marriage to Ellen.

Eddie Rickenbacker – the famous world war ace and good friend of both Winchell and Runyon.

And Captain John Gill, who will pilot the plane, which will take off from La Guardia Field, and fly over the New York skyline.

Winchell also has a letter which he promised he would not open and read until Runyon's death.

The seating of the plane is like a small cargo aircraft where people sit across from each other, facing each other.

Damon Jr. and his wife are on one side – and Rickenbacker and Winchell on the other.

As the plane takes off and noses upward the first few moments find the passengers extremely quiet, and all thinking their own thoughts.

After a few moments, Winchell breaks the silence by announcing that he has an unopened letter from Damon which he will now read. He displays the envelope and pulls out the letter. And with hands that are slightly trembling, he holds the letter and reads.

Dear Walter: Words cannot express what your friendship has meant to me. I was always aware of the sacrifices you made - but my small-town nature would not allow me to show the deep appreciation I felt.

Winchell puts one hand over his face as though hiding his tears. Damon Jr.'s wife also has tear-filled eyes. Winchell slowly continues:

Please tell Damon Junior . . .

As Damon Jr. hears his name, his eyes start filling. His wife is openly sobbing.

...that I'm sorry I wasn't a better father. I did love him – but some of us are just not cut out to be parents.
By the way, Walter, if you ever run into Patrice – now you can tell her I never stopped loving her.
Please don't feel that my departing is a great loss – 'cause I've always felt that life is just a journey, and in death you continue on. So don't shed any tears for me 'cause I'm not complaining.
I never believed my words would give me a life that was only known to kings. And deep down inside – I never believed I really deserved it. There are a few things I learned along the way – that a guy with a typewriter wields an awful lot of power, and it's important to be kind.
I found that an irresponsible reporter in front of a typewriter can do more damage than a drunken surgeon in an operating room. Maybe that's why I wrote about the losers. I felt those were the stories that should be told. And maybe my small pat on the back would let them know somebody cares. 'Cause when the world has forgotten – the guy that's down to the cloth will remember who came up with that hot bowl

of soup.

So give my thanks to the newspaper game for the pat on the back they gave to a busted-out kid from Kansas, and thank them for giving me a life. Well, Walter, there's no use of my rambling on, I know you know what I feel. So as they say in our racket – I guess that's thirty for now.

So long, Walter – I love you.

Signed, Damon.

Winchell folds the letter and puts it in his pocket. Rickenbacker then slides a window open. Damon Jr. and his wife come over to Winchell's side – and Winchell turns the urn over outside the window...the ashes slowly scatter.

Winchell quietly says, "So long, Damon. I love you – and I'll never forget you."

And Winchell never did forget Runyon. He raised thirty-two million dollars for the Damon Runyon Cancer Fund which he turned over to universities and medical research centers. And not one penny was ever taken out for expenses. And to this day support still comes in.

The Fund even had its own slogan – "Arrest Cancer – It's Wanted for Murder." Winchell also promised that any newspaperman or woman stricken with this ill-fated disease would always receive hospitalization and treatment free of charge. And it's ironic that in Nineteen Seventy-Two, at the age of Seventy-four, Walter Winchell died of cancer.

Yes, Winchell and Runyon, two men who blazed a trail in the most unforgettable era of the 20th century.

THE END